Underground Homeschool Field Guide

An Illustrated Dialogue Journal

By Rechara Landers Groves, M.S.Ed.

UNDERGROUND HOMESCHOOL™

EMPOWERING ENRICHING EDUCATION ™

Scan this QR code to visit our website for updates, resources, and animated chapter previews!

www.undergroundhomeschool.com

For permissions, inquiries, or licensing requests, please contact:
hello@undergroundhomeschool.com
www.undergroundhomeschool.com

Cover and interior design by Rechara Landers Groves
Printed in the United States of America
First edition, 2025
ISBN: 979-8-9992554-2-6

For my daughters.
You are my dream.
And to my loving husband, Paul–
you made this 'life is but a dream' come true.

Acknowledgements

To my parents, thank you for grounding me in faith, strength, and possibility. Your example laid the foundation for everything I've become—as a mother, a teacher, and a dreamer. To my brothers, thank you for always believing in my voice, even before I found it on the page. Your support has always echoed louder than any doubt. And to the homeschool mothers who walked this path beside me—and to the ones I've met along the way— thank you for your friendship, your wisdom, and your unwavering belief in this calling. Your courage, creativity, and community made this journey feel less like isolation and more like revolution. I'm grateful for every shared resource, whispered prayer, field trip chat, and unspoken moment of solidarity. We share the same heart, and that shared heartbeat has made the journey lighter, bolder, and full of grace.

Acknowledgment of Voices and Inspiration

Select quotes throughout this book are drawn from the public words of leaders, educators, and changemakers including Marva Collins, Shirley Chisholm, Michelle Obama, and Bob Marley. Their insights continue to inspire generations of learners, families, and freedom seekers.

Preface

Underground Homeschool: Empowering Enriching Education

Maybe your family is considering homeschool for one reason or another. Maybe the public school system isn't meeting the needs of your learner. Or maybe you're simply in search of a more connected, liberating way to educate—one where your child's voice, curiosity, and growth are the priority.

Homeschooling, I've found, is the most liberating journey of discovery—not only for my children, but for myself. It's a quantum of experiential learning. It's hands-on. It's heart-led. And it has expanded, nurtured, and satiated my purpose in ways I never expected.

I'm Rechara Landers Groves, an institutionally trained educator turned homeschool mom. I've worked inside traditional classrooms and studied pedagogical theory. I know the strengths and limitations of the system—and I knew I could create something more robust, more meaningful, and more joyful for my three daughters. So I went underground, so to speak, and began crafting a personalized, research-informed educational journey that honored both who my children are and the kind of childhood I wanted them to have.

This book is not a prescription—it's an invitation.

Each chapter shares a lived experience from our homeschool days, a life lesson wrapped in narrative, research reflection, and practical inspiration. The format is modeled after the dialogue journal, a tool shown to support deep reflection and communication in both traditional and alternative educational settings[1,2]. In this book, I write to you—and at the end of each chapter, I invite you to write back through prompts designed to guide your own reflection.

Why a dialogue format? Because homeschooling isn't linear—it's layered. It isn't one-size-fits-all—it's individual. And perhaps most importantly, it isn't just about content—it's about connection.

Just as dialogue journals have been shown to deepen learning, build identity, and improve teacher-student relationships[1,2], my hope is that this book becomes a space for your reflection and growth. It's for new homeschoolers, seasoned ones, and everyone in between. Whether your approach is traditional, interest-led, unschooling, game-based, or hybrid—there's space for you here.

You'll find chapters on everything from science dissections and surfing trips to curriculum planning and chess games. You'll meet my daughters, hear their voices, and see how ordinary days turned into extraordinary growth.

Every scene shared here—whether joyful, gritty, or bold—is rooted in actual events. The characters and dialogue are drawn from real life, though I have used pseudonyms for my children and others to preserve their privacy. Some moments have been gently condensed or restructured for clarity, but the essence of each story remains true.

These are the lived experiences that taught my daughters—and myself—how to think critically, love deeply, and move bravely through the world.

You don't need to replicate our journey—you only need the courage to start your own.

This book is a window into the kind of education that cultivates not only intellect, but also courage, compassion, and curiosity. In a time when advanced technology can answer questions in seconds, this book facilitates learning what digital platforms can't teach: lessons in human experiences.

And while these methods are grounded in real-world practice, they work in tandem with innovation. When paired with technological tools and programming, this heart-centered approach to learning creates a holistic education—one that honors both our humanity and the evolving digital landscape.

May these pages inspire you to trust your instincts, embrace your own rhythm, and reclaim the joy and power of learning at home.

The goal is inspiration. The tool is reflection. The gift is freedom.

Welcome to Underground Homeschool.

1. Denne-Bolton, Sandra. "The Dialogue Journal: A Tool for Building Better Writers." English Teaching Forum 51, no. 2 (2013): 2–11.

2. Garmon, M. A. (2001). The benefits of dialogue journals: What prospective teachers say. Teacher Education Quarterly, 28(4), 37–50.

CHAPTERS

"Success doesn't come from what you do occasionally, it comes from what you do consistently."

~ MICHELLE OBAMA

A DAY IN THE HOMESCHOOL LIFE

EMBRACING RHYTHM OVER RIGIDITY

A DAY IN THE HOMESCHOOL LIFE

EMBRACING RHYTHM OVER RIGIDITY

What does homeschool really look like—at home?

This was a question I found myself reflecting on one slow morning as we eased into our Fall Break. It wasn't a day packed with curriculum checklists or formal lessons. It was a day that started late—at least by our standards.

The girls are usually up before 7, following the same laminated checklist posted in the bathroom:

Brush teeth. Check.
Wash face. Check.
Clean sink. Get dressed. Tidy room. Check, check, check!

Then they come out for breakfast—toast and eggs, instant oatmeal, a smoothie, or cereal. But on this particular morning? Mama was tired. I didn't roll out of bed until 8:30.

And let me tell you—if anybody claims being home with kids, homeschooling or not, isn't a full-time, overtime job... they lyin'. Still, even with the slow start, something beautiful unfolded.

Before my feet even touched the floor, I reached for my phone and tapped the Bluetooth speaker. The soft melody of our morning playlist filled the house. It's a small act that carries big weight in our homeschool rhythm. The sound of music drifting through the house is our way of saying: it's time to begin. We don't need bells or a formal schedule—just the comfort of cues we've built into our days. The kids, recognizing the signal, would begin to move. But today, they were already ahead of me.

When I finally emerged, stretching and blinking into the day, I stopped in my tracks. There they were. Already dressed. Already smiling. Already working.

Ari looked up from her coloring sheet and grinned. "Look, Mama—green four!" she shouted as she scribbled over the letter and number of the day.

Lizzy had her head bent over her planner, circling her activities for the day, journaling her positive affirmation quote. "I am capable of whatever I put my mind to."

June was busy cutting and pasting, her tongue slightly out in deep concentration. She'd matched all the 'ch' sounds to the pictures. "Look Mommy! "Ch" cheese, "ch" church, "ch" cherry! "

I stood still in the kitchen, heart full and eyes wide.

I watched as they all sat at the kitchen table, beginning their "morning work." That's what we call the warm-up activities that they can complete independently to foster a posture of autonomous productivity. This wasn't a special day or a performance for a camera. It was the natural result of making learning our lifestyle. That moment wasn't about compliance. It was about confidence. Ownership. Joy.

Our days often begin with a flexible routine rooted in predictability. We don't stick to rigid times (tried that), but we do have rhythms. Mornings usually start with breakfast and some movement—either light stretching, a dance break, or a few laps in the backyard to get the wiggles out. Then we circle up in the living room for "morning meeting." This is our time to connect spiritually, emotionally, and academically. We share our intentions for the day, go over any plans or projects, and sometimes do a short devotion or gratitude journal. After that, the day unfolds like music on shuffle—each moment part of a greater harmony.

After that, the learning blocks begin. We rotate between group lessons and independent work depending on the day and the subject. The dining table becomes a math lab. The couch, a reading nest. The floor, a discovery zone with puzzles and games scattered like breadcrumbs of learning. And a computer station for independent technology-based learning.

And if I've managed it well, I even get a chance to meal-prep in between the day's activities. Even the kitchen played its part.

"Mom, can I stir the soup while I wait for you to check my work?" Lizzy called from the stove.

"Sure," I said, handing her the spoon, adjusting her arm, and guiding her rotation.

What's important is not just where we learn—but how we've made learning part of our lifestyle. Because we homeschool, we've embraced a model that integrates education into everything we do. Our children have learned to take initiative, explore their interests, and navigate their day with a sense of autonomy. And on days like this —when I am not even fully awake yet—they still choose learning. They still show up with joy.

That kind of motivation isn't magic. It comes from intentional effort. Over time, we've
built habits that empower independence. We use music to mark transitions, offer visual charts or checklists for daily goals, and give each child ownership over parts of their schedule. We keep supplies organized in labeled bins and baskets so they know where to find what they need. And we reward consistency—not with bribes, but with praise, special privileges, and the satisfaction of mastery.

By midday on this particular day, the house was filled with the smell of kale-lentil soup that I had the chance to prepare, the sound of laughter, and the buzz of productivity. Ari danced past me in a Disney princess costume. June was stretched out on the rug, building the tallest tower with her magnetic tiles. Our home was alive —with movement, with laughter, with learning.

And I? I sat at the kitchen table, coffee in hand, quietly journaling thoughts for this very chapter. It wasn't a flashy day. No experiments. No field trips. No major milestones.
But it was perfect in the way that only ordinary days can be. The kind of day that reminds you why you chose this path in the first place.

Author's Reflection

When we first started homeschooling, I believed I had to recreate school at home—structured schedules, rigid seatwork, constant direction. But what I've come to love most about this journey is how much I've grown in letting go. I've learned to lean into the rhythm of our home and trust in the systems we've created.

Watching my daughters take initiative without prompting was one of those proud, quiet moments where everything I've poured into them reflected right back. It reminded me that our homeschool isn't defined by academic rigor alone—it's about cultivating lifelong learners who are confident, self-driven, and joyful. What I've built is a system that offers structure without rigidity—expectation wrapped in trust.

According to the principles of Universal Design for Learning, learning environments should be arranged to promote independence, flexible access, and student autonomy.[3] That's what our home has become. The couch is a reading nook, the kitchen a lab, the music a cue. Our space doesn't look like a classroom—but it functions like one, with routines that guide and empower.

And it's not just the setup—it's the feedback. I no longer wait for worksheets to affirm learning. I notice growth in the way a child remembers where to find the tape, initiates a journal entry, or encourages her sister through a new task.

This is formative assessment in motion—ongoing, informal, and rooted in responsive guidance.[4]

The music in the morning? That's not just ambiance—it's a self-regulation cue, a habit loop that supports autonomy and focus. As Wilson and Conyers affirm, metacognitive cues and strategies can help students develop not just knowledge, but the confidence to direct their own learning.[5] That's what I'm seeing in my daughters—and in myself.

Our days are not always picture-perfect. There are meltdowns, interruptions, and times we throw the whole plan out the window. But even those days teach us something valuable. On the good days—like this one—I get to witness what happens when intentional design meets personal growth: kids who learn because they love to, not because they're told to. The reward isn't in the productivity—it's in the agency. That's what makes a typical homeschool day extraordinary.

3. CAST. (2018). Universal Design for Learning guidelines version 2.2. http://udlguidelines.cast.org

4. Wiliam, D., & Black, P. (1998). Inside the black box: Raising standards through classroom assessment. Phi Delta Kappan, 80(2), 139–148.

5. Wilson, D., & Conyers, M. (2016). Teaching students to drive their brains: Metacognitive strategies, activities, and lesson ideas. ASCD.

Reader Reflections

Take a moment to reflect on your daily rhythms. What does a "day in the homeschool life" look like in your home right now? What cues or traditions have you built into your learning environment that support independence and joy?

Have your children ever surprised you by stepping into leadership or initiating their own learning? What habits or values might have made that possible?

READER REFLECTIONS

Think about your home's learning environment. How is it arranged to encourage creativity, independence, or comfort? What's working well? What would you love to adjust?

"Culture does not make people. People make culture."

~ **CHIMAMANDA NGOZI ADICHIE**

ROOTED IN LEGACY
LOVE
TEACH
IDENTITY GROWS DEEP WHEN
IT'S PLANTED IN TRUTH

Rooted in Legacy

Identity Grows Deep When Its Planted in Truth

From the very beginning, I knew that teaching my daughters their history—our history—couldn't be a footnote. It had to be a foundation. And we didn't need textbooks to start—we needed truth, experience, and presence.

Homeschooling gave us the gift of time and intention. Time to travel. To read. To reflect. To walk where our ancestors once stood, fought, and persevered.

When we moved to Memphis, reunited with a host of cousins, uncles, aunts, and distant relatives, our first discovery began with a stroll down Beale Street—not for barbecue or souvenirs, but to hear the echoes of a cultural revolution. On the Memphis Blues Music Trail walking tour, we followed the sounds of B.B. King, W.C. Handy, and the soul-stirring pulse of a people whose resilience turned pain into rhythm. Each historical placard became a lesson. The music wasn't just entertainment—it was testimony.

At the end of the tour, I crouched next to my then-seven-year-old. "What did you learn, sweetheart?"

She paused, thinking. "Music brought Black people and White people together," she said softly.

While in Memphis, we also learned about Slave Haven—a real home that had served as a stop on the Underground Railroad. We didn't visit the house, believing our daughters were still quite young for its intensity. But we acknowledged it. We honored it. And we discussed what it meant to open your home, your life, your safety, to help someone else escape bondage.

"That's what legacy means," I told them. "Risking something... to free someone."

Eventually, job changes brought us back to the Sunshine State of Florida. In St. Augustine, our journey continued with visits to the Lincolnville Museum, where exhibits celebrated Black excellence, education, and entrepreneurship in Florida. Just minutes away, we walked the grounds of the ACCORD Civil Rights Museum. One of our stops was the former home of Dr. Robert B. Hayling, a local dentist and courageous activist who opened his doors—and his life—to Dr. Martin Luther King Jr. and fellow civil rights leaders. It's humbling to stand on the same streets where meetings that shaped the movement were once held, right in our backyard.

And then there are moments when the learning happens in quieter ways.

The girls sat at the kitchen table, coloring quietly while the television broadcast history. Kamala Harris placed her hand on the Bible and took the oath of office.

Lizzy whispered, "She looks like me."

Later, we would meet Black authors at book fairs and listen to stories from Ghanaian mythology. Whether wearing matching kente cloth for Kwanzaa or sketching Harriet Tubman's face from a museum display, I watched my daughters not just learn history —but locate themselves inside of it.

We honored Kwanzaa by reading books on the tradition and attending local celebrations at our African American Cultural Society—where Shirley Chisholm served in retirement before her passing. The original "Unbought and Unbossed."

In addition to her historic 1972 presidential run, we learned about her tireless advocacy for educational policies that ensure equal access to quality learning for all children, especially those from underprivileged backgrounds. We walked where she once served, letting her legacy speak through the very space she helped shape.

We also created our own atmosphere grounded in the principles. The seven values gave us words for what we were already living: unity (Umoja), collective work and responsibility (Ujima), and purpose (Nia). These weren't new concepts in our home— they were simply now being named.

At Fort Mose, the first legally sanctioned free Black settlement in what would become the United States, my girls stood where freedom had been fiercely claimed. We walked slowly through the interpretive center. They paused at each panel. They ran their fingers over worn timelines and traced artifacts with awe. We didn't rush. We lingered.

One year, we traveled to Washington D.C. and spent hours in the Smithsonian National Museum of African American History and Culture. I watched my oldest, Lizzy, read aloud from an original draft of the Declaration of Independence, her eyes wide with dismay as she stumbled over the line referencing "a market where men should be bought and sold." She looked up at me—not for answers, but for affirmation. She had found her own truth in the contradiction.

And I nodded, acknowledging its wrongness. This country's story includes horrors and shame, no matter how often it's erased or reframed. And in that museum—in that sacred space filled with resistance, resilience, rhythm, and remembrance—our presence was undeniable.

Black history isn't a chapter. It's the context. It's the soul of our story.

Author's Reflection

So much of what we teach our children shapes how they see themselves in the world. Growing up, I rarely saw my identity reflected in textbooks. Black history was confined to one month, one chapter, one hero. But I refuse to pass down that emptiness. Homeschooling has allowed me to intentionally center culture, identity, and historical truth—not as enrichment, but as foundational learning.

And research supports this path. According to King, Black history education must move beyond narratives of trauma and oppression to cultivate what he calls Black historical consciousness—a framework that allows students to see themselves as agents of history, not just victims of it.[6] This approach uplifts stories of achievement, resistance, and legacy, allowing learners to locate themselves inside the narrative, not outside of it. I see this every time my daughters trace an artifact, pause at a timeline, or connect with content in a personal, powerful way.

I'm not raising children to fit a prescribed narrative. I'm helping them build their own—rooted in truth, not omission; legacy, not loss.

And this isn't just about identity—it's also about good instructional practice. The Florida Department of Education's Effective Practices framework highlights the importance of motivational competency and culturally responsive learning environments that reflect students' lived experiences. When children see themselves in the content, their engagement, achievement, and self-efficacy increase.[7] That's what I witnessed at Fort Mose. In the Smithsonian galleries. In the simple moment when my daughter whispered, "She looks like me."

When our children are grounded in their history, they walk taller. They don't just memorize names—they carry the stories. They speak from a place of understanding. They recognize themselves as part of a lineage of resilience and excellence. This chapter of our learning isn't a seasonal unit—it's a lifelong worldview. We aren't just homeschooling for academics. We're homeschooling to raise children who are rooted, ready, and radiant with purpose.

Black History isn't optional. It's essential.

6. King, L. J. (2023). Teaching through Black history: An overview of Black historical consciousness. ASSERT: The Journal of Educational Leadership and Praxis, 3(1), 49–64. https://assertjournal.com/index.php/assert/article/view/61/182

7. Florida Department of Education. (2022). Effective instructional practices to support student engagement and motivation. Retrieved from https://www.fldoe.org

Reader Reflections

How are you creating space for your children to explore identity, legacy, and justice? What books, films, or experiences might support that journey?

What would it look like to integrate Black history—or any cultural heritage—into everyday learning, not just a single unit?

Reader Reflections

If you could design a field trip to help a child experience their identity through history, where would you go and why?

"It takes a village to raise a child."

~ AFRICAN PROVERB

IT TAKES A VILLAGE
HOMESCHOOL
MOM
INSPIRE
LEAD
TEACH
FOSTERING COMMUNITY AND
COLLABORATION

It Takes a Village

Fostering Community and Collaboration

When people think of homeschooling, they often imagine a child at the kitchen table, isolated from the world, parents quietly orchestrating lessons in a bubble. But our experience has been the opposite. Homeschooling opened us up to a wider, richer community—one that reflects the best of collaboration, generosity, and shared growth.

We didn't do this alone. From the earliest days of our journey, we leaned into the village. After each move, the peripheral search for connection began. We met people at library story times, on playground benches, and during swim lessons at the YMCA. Sometimes, we were brave enough to type "local homeschool group" into a social media search bar and show up to a new group's park day with nervous smiles and hopeful hearts.

Other homeschooling families became our co-teachers, field trip partners, co-op collaborators, and often, dear friends. Together, we pieced together a mosaic of experiences that expanded far beyond the four walls of our home.

Some of our most joyful learning moments happened not during a formal lesson, but in the wild spaces between structure and spontaneity; during a hike through the arboretum, gazing up at the cosmos at a planetarium show, or spontaneous poolside gathering.

One sunny day in Memphis, my two closest homeschool mom friends and I decided to gather our collective eight kids for a bike ride around the lake. Some of our children hadn't yet mastered balance or confidence in riding. There were tricycles wobbling, training wheels clicking, and tiny legs pumping on balance bikes. Laughter echoed across the water as kids called out encouragement.

"You've got it, Ari!" one friend's son shouted, cheering her along.

"Wait for me!" June giggled, trying to catch up on her pink training-wheel cruiser.

Lizzy zoomed past with a proud grin. "I'm gonna do the whole loop without stopping!"

It wasn't a science lesson. But it was learning through play—about grit, about courage, about community.

Our homeschool community was made up of families from all walks of life—different backgrounds, beliefs, and teaching styles. Yet we were bound by the same heartbeat: a commitment to raising confident, curious, and grounded children. We traded lesson ideas, passed down curriculum, hosted history presentations and science projects, and carpooled to classes and events.

One field day we studied marine biology together at the estuary. The kids wore water shoes and wide eyes as they took turns with the field nets, scooping up seagrass and tiny fish. A scavenger hunt led them through ecosystems, notebooks in hand, soaking in every detail.

I was so impressed that June would later remember that day so vividly. “June, what do you remember most about that trip?”

She didn’t hesitate in her response. “Everything! Pulling the net, picking up the crabs, seeing a baby sea turtle swim up to us. And did you know estuaries have both salt and freshwater? It’s called brackish,” she explained.

With our homeschool friends, we explored herpetology at a nature center, dug into the science of light and shadow, studied dinosaurs and constellations at the Museum of Science and History. Every lesson deepened through shared experience.

One of the most beautiful things was watching my daughters form lasting friendships that didn’t rely on being in the same grade or classroom. These friendships were rooted in shared interests, mutual respect, and time spent in meaningful interaction. They learned to lead, to listen, to compromise, and to include.

Community also meant that I didn’t have to do everything alone. There were veteran moms who mentored me, co-op leaders who shared the administrative weight, and friends who’d show up with extra snacks or bug spray for when things got itchy. We created a network of support where everyone contributed and everyone belonged.

Homeschooling can be incredibly rewarding—but it can also be lonely without the right connections. That’s why we prioritized building community. We looked for the helpers, and we became the helpers. We built a life where friendship and education were inseparable.

And that has made all the difference.

Author's Reflection

Looking back, what made our homeschool journey flourish wasn't just the materials or the method—it was the people. As Neuman and Guterman highlight in their qualitative study, homeschooling families often embrace a worldview that prioritizes meaningful relationships, flexibility, and connection as educational cornerstones.[8] That has certainly been true for us. It wasn't simply about removing our children from traditional school structures—it was about surrounding them with a village of people who saw their value and supported their growth.

Our co-op friends, park day playmates, and fellow field trip families weren't just companions—they were co-educators in a larger learning ecosystem. Guterson emphasizes the power of parental intentionality in shaping environments that foster self-directed learning and authentic peer engagement.[9] In our experience, that looked like kids of all ages solving problems together, teaching each other new skills, and growing in empathy as they moved through shared projects and play. It looked like moms exchanging tips while they set up picnic lunches, kissed booboos, and watched the children play, supportive dads bringing the muscle and masculinity for our young men to emulate, and mentors offering both academic support and heartfelt encouragement.

The phrase "it takes a village" isn't just poetic—it's pedagogical. In a homeschool context, the village becomes a flexible, child-centered network that supports learning through trust, community, and shared vision. Whether large or small, your village helps hold you steady on this journey. For us, it created space to thrive—space for my daughters to form multi-age friendships, for me to find solidarity and strength, and for our homeschool to be not only functional, but joyful and expansive. The beauty of it all is that these connections are not accidental; they're built with intention. And as research affirms, it is this intention—paired with a willingness to walk the road together—that transforms education into a truly communal endeavor.

8. Neuman, A., & Guterman, O. (2017). The clash of two worldviews: A qualitative comparison between school teachers and homeschooling parents' attitudes toward education. Issues in Educational Research, 27(4), 1-19. https://www.iier.org.au/iier27/neuman.html

9. Guterson, D. (2018). The role of the parent in the education of gifted students. In S. Pfeiffer (Ed.), Handbook of Giftedness in Children (2nd ed., pp. 297-311). Springer. https://doi.org/10.1007/978-3-319-77004-8_19

Reader Reflections

Describe your homeschool "village."Who are the people that make your homeschool journey lighter, richer, or more joyful? What gifts do they bring to your life and learning?

Do your children have peers or mentors they connect with regularly? What kinds of friendships are being formed through your educational path?

Reader Reflections

How are you nurturing community right now? Are there local co-ops, online groups, or informal meet-ups that you can join or help build?

Reflect on a time when another family or friend supported your homeschool journey. How did that impact your experience or your child's learning?

"Once you learn to read, you will be forever free."

~ FREDRICK DOUGLAS

THE LIBRARY
LIFELINE
BAKING
LITERACY WITHIN
THEIR REACH

The Library Lifeline

Literacy Within Their Reach

There is something sacred about stepping into a library. The quiet rustle of pages turning, the soft creak of a rolling book cart, the hushed conversations at the help desk—it's a world of calm that pulses with possibility. For our homeschool family, the library wasn't just a place to check out books. It was a cornerstone of our curriculum, a sanctuary for imagination, and a true literacy lifeline.

From the time my girls were toddlers, weekly library visits became part of our rhythm. It wasn't just something to do to get out of the house—they were events.

As a lively storyteller began the opening lines of a fairytale, "Once upon a time..."

The room fell still, except for wide eyes and bouncing knees, and the children were transported into a whimsical make-believe adventure. Afterwards, there was singing, dancing, and crafts with cotton balls and googly eyes and glue sticks that never quite stayed shut.

In those early years, it wasn't just about choosing books. Each visit was about being immersed in a full sensory experience that nurtured their love of language.

As they grew, each child found her niche.

"Can we stay just a little longer?" Lizzy would ask as she inched toward the graphic novels.

"I want to finish my puppet show!" Ari pleaded. The youngest made a beeline for the puppet corner, pulling out props and retelling stories from memory in a flurry of dramatic voices and giggles.

"I still need one more baking book," June said, nestled beside the early reader shelves, carefully selecting every Step 1 baking-themed book she could find.

These weren't just cute habits. They were the building blocks of literacy.

Library events grew into social highlights. My daughters eagerly anticipated seasonal presentations and book clubs with the librarians—some of whom knew their names and favorite book series. One afternoon, as we walked in, the librarian waved us over.

“I saved something for you,” she whispered to Lizzy, pulling a brand-new Babysitters Club Graphic novel from behind the desk.

“It’s not even on the shelves yet,” she said with a wink.

Lizzy clutched it to her chest, eyes wide.

“Thank you! I was waiting for this one!”

That moment—being seen, known, remembered—made my daughter feel like the library belonged to her. And in a way, it did.

The library offered access to thousands of books without the pressure of purchasing. It gave my daughters the freedom to explore genres, authors, and topics at their own pace. Some days we left with twenty books, only for half to be returned unread. And that was okay—because the freedom to choose was part of the learning process. And the most precious moments came when we read together—curled up on the couch or sprawled on the floor, trading pages and voices.

As the girls grew, so did our use of the library. It became a launchpad for whole units of study—biographies for Women’s History Month, astronomy books for our space unit, cookbooks to support our baking experiments. We borrowed DVDs and audiobooks for car schooling, STEM kits for hands-on exploration, and even laptops for digital literacy practice.

As a parent and educator, I came to view the library as more than a resource. It was a co-teacher and companion. It filled in the literary gaps, sparked new directions, and transformed literacy from a static skill into a vibrant, living experience. Even in the digital age, it was the placc—the welcoming smiles, the quiet nooks, the magic of unexpected discovery— where a child sees that books are everywhere—and that those books are for them— and a lifetime of literacy takes root. And blooms.

Author's Reflection

The library has been one of our greatest educational assets—and not just for the books. It has represented freedom, curiosity, and access. At times when our homeschool budget was stretched thin, it offered abundance without cost. We didn't have to sacrifice literacy development or exposure to new ideas. The library provided it all—quietly, generously, and consistently.

It was here, among the shelves, that my children became readers—not because they had to, but because they wanted to. That distinction matters. According to Schunk and Zimmerman, fostering reading motivation through autonomy, choice, and meaningful access is key to long-term literacy growth.[10] Every trip to the library supported those goals. Whether it was choosing their own stories or discovering a surprise author tucked in the stacks, my daughters experienced reading as empowerment.

As a parent-educator, I also came to rely on the library for instructional support. From thematic collections to leveled readers, audiobooks to STEM kits, it gave us flexible tools to meet diverse learning needs—exactly the kind of responsive support emphasized by the Florida Center for Reading Research in their guidance on effective literacy instruction.[11]

Libraries are more than repositories of books—they are co-teachers in our homeschool journey. They hold the tools, the inspiration, and the access that make a literacy-rich life possible. The library helped me meet my children where they were, nurture their interests, and extend learning far beyond a textbook. It taught them that reading is not just an academic requirement, but a gateway to curiosity and confidence.

If you're homeschooling without a library card, you're missing out on one of the most research-backed sustaining resources available. In our home, the library wasn't just a resource. It was a lifeline.

10. Schunk, D. H., & Zimmerman, B. J. (2012). Motivation and self-regulated learning: Theory, research, and applications. In J. T. Guthrie et al. (Eds.), Best practices in motivation and literacy instruction (pp. 214–226). Guilford Press.

11. Florida Center for Reading Research. (2022). Assessments to inform instruction overview. https://fcrr.org/resources

Reader Reflections

In what ways can, or has, the library supported your child's learning, curiosity, or creativity—beyond just borrowing books?

Make a list of hidden gems your local library may offer that you want to explore. Are there digital resources, themed programs, or homeschool meet-ups—that could enrich your learning?

Reader Reflections

And if your access to libraries is limited, what alternatives might help you recreate that spirit of curiosity and access in your home or community?

"The essence of teaching is to make learning contagious, to have one idea spark another."

~ MARVA COLLINS

CURRICULUM ON A MISSION
TEACHER
CURRICULUM MANUAL
Learning Games
SCIENCE
GRAMMAR
MATH
INNOVATIVE PLANNING FOR MULTIPLE LEARNERS

Curriculum on a Mission

Innovative Planning for Multiple Learners

Curriculum planning in a homeschool with multiple learners isn't just about choosing books—it's a dance of logistics, creativity, and love. Each child has a different pace, a different spark, a different learning style. I quickly learned that what works beautifully for one might frustrate another. So I adapted, layered, and built our educational rhythm piece by piece.

But that certainly did not happen overnight. I've tried so many curricula. Full-time online school with daily Zooms. Complete boxed sets for every core subject. A-la-carte computer apps. A-la-carte manipulatives. Faith-based, family-style, workbook-heavy, game-centered—you name it. Some things stuck. Others fell by the wayside.

Too rigorous. Not rigorous enough. Too expensive. Too time-consuming. Boring.

I did all that legwork to learn this: I didn't need a pre-designed boxed curriculum stuffed with standard information. I needed connection, flexibility, and strategy over stress.

The secret weapon? Resourcefulness.

I didn't need to buy a separate program for each child—I needed to layer levels and stretch resources across age groups. I learned to level up or level down the same topic. If we were studying compound words, my Pre-K child worked with picture cards and matching games, while my kindergartener used cut-and-glue worksheets, and my 2nd grader applied the words in full sentences and narratives. One concept, three approaches. We played the same card game together, just with different expectations.

"I'm going to write a sentence with 'sunflower'!" Lizzy thought outloud one day.

"Ok! June, can you find the two words inside 'sunflower'?" I challenged.

June grinned, holding up a flashcard. "Sun and flower!"

When studying thematic units, each learner receives texts at their individual reading levels with questioning and activities to match abilities. Lizzy may be able to give written responses to prompts on ancient Aztec culture, while Ari can handle coloring the characters of a Mayan calendar while she listens to a text on the topic read aloud.

Some thematic, family-style curricula have this differentiation built in. For a more manual approach, today there are so many AI tools and applications that make differentiating instruction attainable, and available, right at your fingertips.

Some of our best curriculum choices didn't come from catalogs—but from Goodwill bins and library backrooms. I cannot tell you how many times I've walked out of a thrift store with a $1–$3 gem—full spelling kits, barely used workbooks, science experiments, educational board games. Each item felt like a little donation from an anonymous educator cheering me on.

We also used free public resources as part of our core curriculum. Local library story times turned into literacy anchors. Museum memberships became a key part of our science and history experience—we squeezed every bit of learning out of every exhibit, hands-on station, and presentation. State and national park materials added a real-world spark to our studies: pamphlets and maps for geography, landform boards for earth science, and nature scavenger hunts for biology.

"Can I bring this map home?" June asked during a hike, gripping a pamphlet like treasure.

"Absolutely," I smiled. "We can use that in our geography lessons."

Our planning system is fluid but intentional. We create a yearly vision and then break it down by quarter. I use color-coded planning sheets, printed goal trackers, and a simple daily planner for each child. I don't stress if plans shift—flexibility is part of our design. We school year-round, taking breaks when needed and diving deep when inspiration strikes.

We began one year with a unit of community helpers, which led to a series of field trips to local businesses and services. Another time, a weather event triggered an impromptu unit on hurricanes and meteorology. When their questions take us somewhere, I follow. And when they're ready to move on, we pivot, keeping reading, grammar, and arithmetic as a staple.

I've learned to trust the rhythm of interest, stretch every resource, and build from curiosity. Our curriculum may not be fancy—but it is intentional, integrated, and ours.

Author's Reflection

I used to think a good homeschool meant having a shelf of matching curriculum sets, carefully scheduled lesson plans, and daily checklists. But experience—and my children—taught me otherwise. Planning for multiple learners required not more materials, but more strategy, flexibility, and trust in the process. While there are many, many well organized curriculum programs and supplements that do meet the needs of multiple learners, with homeschooling there's no pressure to go "all in" with one right away. We have space and time to explore what works.

One of the most transformative shifts came when I embraced the principles of curriculum compacting. As Reis and Renzulli suggest, compacting allows learners to skip unnecessary repetition and instead focus on enriched, engaging tasks that challenge them appropriately.[12] It gave me permission to move beyond grade-level expectations and lean into what actually ignited my children's curiosity. Whether that meant condensing a unit that had already been mastered or letting a spontaneous science lesson bloom from a weather event, I found more learning happened when I released the pressure to "cover it all."

I also found affirmation in the Maker Model, which encourages educators to differentiate the curriculum by adjusting content, process, product, and learning environment.[13] That's what I do when I level up a topic like compound words across my learners—using games, crafty activities, sentence writing, and thematic posters all on the same table. I was modifying the process and product without intentionally doing something "research-based," but intentionally individualizing the instruction.

Our homeschool doesn't always run on precision. But it runs with purpose. And that purpose is to build a flexible, layered, life-connected education—one that meets each child where they are and allows them to grow confidently from that place.

Planning for multiple learners isn't a juggling act—it's an opportunity to cultivate depth, creativity, and collaboration. I no longer see it as a challenge to overcome, but as a strength in our rhythm. With the right mindset, strategic use of free and frugal resources, and intentional pacing, a diverse learning environment becomes not only possible—but powerful.

12. Reis, S. M., & Renzulli, J. S. (1992). Curriculum compacting: The complete guide to modifying the regular curriculum for high ability students. Creative Learning Press.

13. Maker, J. C. (1982). Curriculum development for the gifted. Aspen Systems Corporation.

Reader Reflections

How do you currently approach curriculum planning in your homeschool or learning space?

In what ways can you teach a single topic across multiple levels in your home or classroom?

Reader Reflections

Brainstorm a list of learning goals for your students. Then, research curriculum options that could meet those needs. Bonus if its family oriented!

Make a list of your favorite places to find low-cost or free educational resources. How could you build a lesson using just those?

"Don't let anyone rob you of your imagination, your creativity, or your curiosity."

~ MAE JEMISON

EXPLORING THE UNIVERSE
THE DEPTH AND BREADTH OF THEMATIC MONTHLY UNITS

Exploring the Universe

The Depth and Breadth of Thematic Monthly Units

It started with a simple question: What's beyond the sky?

One cool, clear morning, we sat on the back patio after breakfast, sipping tea and staring upward. Wispy clouds drifted across the blue, and one of my daughters tilted her head toward the sky,

"How high up do the clouds go?" she asked.

Then, after a pause, "What's after that?"

That spark—small, curious, and innocent—ignited an entire month of exploration that would take us far beyond our backyard and deep into the mysteries of the universe.

We declared it: Space Month.

Our kitchen table transformed into Mission Control. The walls filled with constellation charts, solar system cling-ons, and galaxy art pour-painted with glitter and awe. Our library tote strained under the weight of books about planets, astronauts, black holes, and stardust. Even the playlist changed—out went the usual tunes, in came Have Fun Teaching's science playlist including "Moon Song."[14]

Before long, they were singing in the car:

"New moon, waxing crescent, first quarter, waxing gibbous, full moon..."

Lizzy belted it out like a pop star.

"Waning gibbous, last quarter, waning crescent!" June added, drumming on her seat.

Ari chimed in singing her own echo. "These are the phases of the moon...moon... moon!"

Each week had a theme:

Week 1: Our Star, Moon, and Planet – We made interactive flip books illustrating the phases of the moon, and acted out orbit, rotation, and eclipses by spinning around each other in the backyard. The laughter was uncontrollable as they twirled until they fell over in dizzy delight.

Week 2: The Solar System – Using foam balls and paint, we built scaled models and crafted "planet passports" filled with fun facts. We mapped the planets' order with sidewalk chalk across the driveway.

Week 3: Space Exploration – We studied the race to the moon, Mars rovers, and designed our own imaginary missions, complete with hand-drawn crew patches. The girls built a LEGO NASA station and space shuttle with impressive attention to detail.

Week 4: Faraway Stars and Galaxies – Nighttime became magical. We lay on blankets stargazing, identifying constellations and inventing new mythologies for their shapes. Indoors, we created swirling pour-paint galaxy scenes with glittery "space dust" and tiny paper stars.

In the evenings, to wind down before bed, we watched "Cosmos: A Spacetime Odyssey" hosted by Neil deGrasse Tyson. Sure, maybe most of it went over their heads at that elementary age, and maybe they even dozed off, but it was all a part of the immersive family learning experience, enriching each of us in our individual capacities.

Learning didn't stay confined to books and crafts—it became a living, breathing adventure. We ended our month with a field trip to Discovery America Science Center. There, the girls zipped into child-size astronaut suits and trained like space explorers. They crawled through obstacle courses, tasted "space food" (freeze-dried strawberries and ice cream), and practiced slow-motion floating in simulated spaceship rooms.

Then we entered the planetarium. We filed into the dark, dome-shaped room. The lights dimmed. The stars came alive.

As galaxies spiraled above, the girls whispered in awe.

"Look at that nebula," Lizzy gasped.

"The stars are..burning? Wait, is our star burning? Wait, are we going to burn?!" June's voice trembled with wonder.

"Mommy can I sit with you," Ari whispered in the darkness.

We sat still—bodies grounded, hearts suspended.

Sitting beneath the domed ceiling, as stars whirled and shimmered above us, we were transported. The room faded, and we felt suspended in the cosmos—part of something vast, ancient, and stunningly beautiful. It wasn't just a science lesson. It was an invitation into wonder.

The exploration of space themes have continued to be layered in throughout the years. Astronomy is one of those sciences that is never resolved. One year we visited the Kennedy Space Center, the Florida home of NASA. They experienced the thunderous vibrations of lift-off in a launch simulator, clutching the seats in giddy excitement.

They saw spaceships that had actually been in space! And there was a hushed reverence when we sat in the launch control room, and experienced a reenactment of the first rocket launch and felt the tremor, simulating what onlookers would have felt during lift off, as if we were reverencing something holy.

And that feeling has never really left us.

Author's Reflection

What I cherish most about our Space Month wasn't just the facts we memorized or the crafts we made—it was the sense of wonder that filled our home.

Our Space Month wasn't just a thematic unit—it was a gateway to curiosity, creativity, and emotional engagement. When children are immersed in experiences that inspire awe, they remember what they learned and how they felt while learning it. Research shows that awe doesn't just enrich emotional well-being—it actually enhances cognitive processing and promotes deeper learning.[15]

Through the eyes of my children, I was reminded how breathtaking the universe is. How easy it is, as adults, to lose our sense of amazement in the everyday grind. But sitting beside them, watching them spin their own galaxies into being with glue and glitter, I remembered: curiosity is sacred. Wonder is sacred.

Inquiry-based learning, where children ask their own questions and pursue the answers through active exploration, has long been championed as a best practice in science education.[16] And when we paired that with imaginative art, physical movement, and storytelling, it transformed content knowledge into something lasting. According to Harlen and Qualter science learning becomes most powerful when it integrates observation, prediction, reflection, and real-world application—precisely what our month of space study offered.[17]

In the end, Space Month wasn't just about astronomy or black holes. It was about empowerment. My daughters didn't just learn facts about planets—they learned how to seek, question, wonder, and create. They discovered that science isn't locked inside a textbook; it's unfolding all around them. And they weren't just learning content—they were becoming lifelong learners, expanding their hearts and minds toward the infinite.

14. Have Fun Teaching. (2012). The moon song [Video]. YouTube. https://www.youtube.com/watch?v=79M2lSVZiY4

15. Gottlieb, S., Dacher, K., & Oveis, C. (2018). Awe as a pathway to cognitive expansion: The impact of awe on learning and perception. Cognition and Emotion, 32(3), 586–593. https://doi.org/10.1080/02699931.2017.1340268

16. Harlen, W., & Qualter, A. (2014). The Teaching of Science in Primary Schools (6th ed.). Routledge.

17. National Research Council. (2000). Inquiry and the National Science Education Standards: A Guide for Teaching and Learning. The National Academies Press. https://doi.org/10.17226/9596

Reader Reflections

What questions from your child have sparked unexpected deep dives or unit studies?

Is there a subject you personally would love to explore alongside your children—not because you have to teach it, but because you would love to learn it, too.

Reader Reflections

Imagine a new month-long learning theme your family could dive into. What resources, activities, or field trips could make it come alive?

"Science is a way of thinking much more than it is a body of knowledge."

~ CARL SAGAN

EYES WIDE OPEN
F P
T O Z
LENS
HUMAN ANATOMY
CURIOSITY AND COURAGE LEAD TO DISCOVERY

Eyes Wide Open

Curiosity and Courage Lead to Discovery

The room was dim, the black microscope glowing softly beneath their eager faces. Lizzy, Ari, and June leaned in close, captivated by the magnified mystery beneath the lens. Our dining room had transformed into a lab—a space of focus, excitement, and scientific wonder.

Spread across the table was a full exploration dissection kit labeled: The Eye. It came with everything: detailed diagrams, a realistic model, bold-colored instructions, vocabulary flashcards, and booklets filled with rich content. There were no textbooks that day—only tools, curiosity, and the freedom to explore. The science kit promised a journey through biology—and it delivered.

We started indoors, building knowledge piece by piece. Beginning with a song and video in the theme of the unit. I've long accepted that our home will echo with silly educational songs—and I'm grateful for it. Songs like The Eye Anatomy Song by Kids Learning Tube may be a bit quirky, but they offer high-quality lyrical content in a format that sticks.[18]

When my girls belt out, "the crystal clear transparent layer is called the cornea, it lets us see the colored iris everyday..." while bopping around in the living room, I know I got'em hooked. They're engaged.

Then, the girls immersed themselves in the table activities. They took turns reading aloud, matched vocabulary to diagrams, colored detailed images of the cornea, pupil, retina, and lens, and carefully assembled a working eye model. Each layer of the lesson deepened their understanding—and added fuel to their excitement.

They even played optometrist in the living room, covering one eye with a wooden spoon to test their vision on a printed alphabet chart. They tried on old glasses to simulate nearsightedness and watched engaging videos—from the cartoon Dr. Binocs Show, to more technical dissection tutorials.[19]

But the real magic—the moment that would etch itself in memory—happened outside, on the lanai.

Gloved, goggled, and just a little squeamish, the girls stepped up to their challenge: dissecting a cow's eye.

At first, they just stared at it. It was bigger than expected—slick, heavy, and strangely beautiful. Their postures held a flicker of hesitation.

“Are we really doing this?” June asked the trio.

But curiosity conquered hesitation.

Together, they made the first incision. Carefully, deliberately, they sliced through layers, identified the parts, and peeled back the mystery.

“Look! That’s the sclera—look how thick it is!”

“Wait, is that the optic nerve?”

Then came the moment of awe: the lens. A clear, jelly-like orb, lifted gently and held to the sun like a treasure.

Ari gasped. “It looks like a glass marble.”

Lizzy turned it between her fingers. “I can see through it!”

“Can I hold the lens next?” June asked.

It wasn’t just science. It was bravery. It was teamwork. It was real-world anatomy in their hands!

And they were completely captivated.

To close the unit, I scheduled an eye exam for myself—and brought my clip-board-carrying scientists along for the ride. And they weren’t passive observers—they were active learners. They filled out anatomy worksheets in the waiting room, and giggled gleefully when it was their turn to have a seat in the refraction chair.

When the doctor came in, they leaned in, asked questions, and watched the equipment with fascination.

As the optometrist held the ophthalmoscope to my eye, Lizzy asked, “Why does the pupil get bigger when you put those drops in?”

“These drops relax the muscles of the iris so the pupil space will enlarge for me to have a better view inside of the eye,” the doctor answered.

“Can you see the retina?”

“Yes, the light allows me to see all the way to the back of the eye,” the doctor replied.

June asked, “Where is the colorful layer like the one from the cow’s eye that we dissected?”

To which the eye doctor most informatively replied, “Oh, you’re thinking of the tapetum lucidum! Only animals have that iridescent layer to refract light so they can see better at night.“

“Oh! Like when we went trick-or-treating at the Alligator Farm at night, and we shined our light on the water and all the alligator eyes glow in the dark!” Ari recollected.

“Yeah, that was creepy!” June recalled.

The transfer of experiential knowledge is remarkable. They weren’t just learning about eyes. They were seeing themselves as scientists, investigators, and capable young minds deeply connected to the world around them.

It wasn’t just a unit. It was a glimpse into possibility.

Author's Reflection

This experience taught me that science education isn't about having all the right answers—it's about cultivating curiosity and courage. When we give children the tools and the trust to explore real concepts with their senses, they become more than students—they become investigators, thinkers, and creators.

It's not that every lesson has to involve goggles and scalpel blades. It's that every child deserves to feel the spark of deep, engaged learning. The kind of learning that doesn't just fill a page—it fills the room.

What made this unit powerful wasn't just the dissection kit or the trip to the optometrist. It was the interdisciplinary richness, where vocabulary, reading, anatomy, observation, and real-world connection came together in one living, breathing experience. This aligns closely with the Depth and Complexity Framework, which encourages learners to engage across multiple disciplines, ask deep questions, and use the language of the field.[20] My daughters weren't just learning about the eye —they were thinking like scientists.

In our homeschool, hands-on learning is not just a method—it's a mindset. We believe in learning by doing. When my daughters held a cow's eye in their gloved hands, they weren't just memorizing parts—they were discovering them.

Research supports this approach. Hands-on science, including dissection kits, has been shown to enhance student engagement, deepen conceptual understanding, and increase retention of complex content.[21] Kinesthetic learning—using movement and physical interaction—helps learners form stronger neural connections by linking cognitive tasks with bodily action.[22] These methods also support spatial reasoning and abstract thinking, especially in STEM fields.

In our homeschool, science comes to life not because of fancy tools, but because we allow space for wonder. "Eyes Wide Open" wasn't just a title—it became our approach: noticing more, exploring deeper, and connecting learning to the world around us. When our children ask questions and seek answers with their own hands and hearts, that's where true education happens.

18. Kids Learning Tube. (2018). Eye anatomy song [Video]. YouTube. https://www.youtube.com/watch?v=vIZ5GfHO5Qo

19. Peekaboo Kidz. (2015–present). The Dr. Binocs Show [YouTube channel]. YouTube. https://www.youtube.com/@PeekabooKidz

20. Kaplan, S. N. (1996). Depth and complexity: An overview of a framework for thinking. California Department of Education.

21. Holstermann, N., Grube, D., & Bögeholz, S. (2010). Hands-on activities and their influence on students' interest. Research in Science Education, 40(5), 743–757. https://doi.org/10.1007/s11165-009-9142-0

22. Macedonia, M. (2014). Bringing back the body into the mind: The role of sensorimotor activity in second language learning. Frontiers in Psychology, 5, 1407. https://doi.org/10.3389/fpsyg.2014.01407

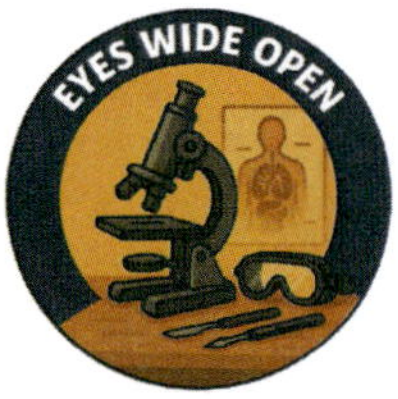

READER REFLECTIONS

Describe a time when a hands-on activity brought a subject to life for your child. What did they remember or retain that surprised you?

In what ways could you stretch yourself as an educator to invite more "doing" into your lessons—especially in science, art, or technical subjects?

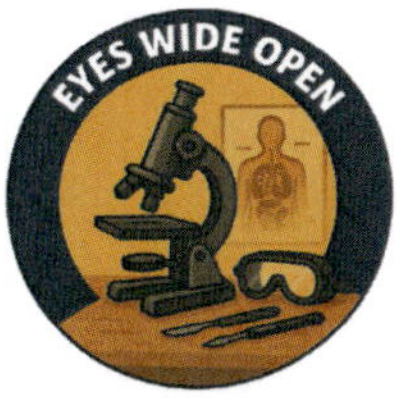

Reader Reflections

How can you pair academic study with real-world exploration—like visits to professionals, live demonstrations, or hands-on resource kits?

Reflect on a time your child overcame reluctance during learning. How did that change how you see them?

"Live in the sunshine, swim in the sea, drink the wild air."

~ RALPH WALDO EMERSON

SURF, SAND, AND SCHOOLING
THE EBB AND FLOW OF EDUCATION

Surf Sand and Schooling

The Ebb and Flow of Educating

The ocean was calling. Not in some poetic, metaphorical way—though it does that too—but in a real, tangible pull we couldn't resist. It was a homeschool day, but instead of pulling out math books and literature guides, we packed towels, notebooks, wetsuits, and sunblock.

The beach was the classroom. It started as a spontaneous idea—the kind homeschooling allows for. We flipped the script: instead of reading about tides, why not ride them? Instead of diagramming the water cycle, why not feel it in motion? Instead of watching nature documentaries, let's go find our own sea creatures in tidepools and shells scattered along the shore.

The forecast was perfect. And the girls were buzzing in the backseat. The 15-minute drive to the coast was filled with anticipation, a playlist of beach tunes, and curious questions flying from the backseat:

"Mom, do you think we'll see dolphins, or jellyfish again?" June anticipated.

"I hope we find a sea star!" Ari exclaimed.

"I wonder if it will be high tide and low tide when we get there?" Lizzy pondered.

By the time we arrived, the air smelled like salt and possibility. The tide flag was green. We unloaded bodyboards, science journals, and a cooler of turkey wraps and fresh fruit. The sound of waves breaking set the rhythm for our day. Learning flowed as naturally as the tides. The girls checked tide charts, predicted wave patterns, and examined sea life in real time. Beneath the umbrella, they peered at sand granules through a talking microscope and compared seaweed to illustrations in our beach exploration guide. My youngest built an entire seaside village from driftwood, shells, and imagination.

Our beach days weren't just academic—they were character-shaping. The most powerful lessons unfolded in the surf.

At surf camp that summer, my oldest daughter tried surfing again after a few rough wipeouts the day before. From the shore, I watched her out in the waist-deep with her trainer. I watched her listen to the master surfer, and could only imagine the instructional and encouraging words she was given as she laid belly-down on her surfboard bobbing up and down with each tiny roll of the waves.

“You can do it. Remember what we practiced. Strong abs, paddle hard, then pop up!” I imagine.

She paddled out. A wave formed behind her. She popped up—stood with bent knees and arms out for balance—wobbled—then splashed down.

She stood for a whole three seconds! And I watched her trainor cheer with both arms pumping that she'd caught her first big one!

She tried again and again, each time rising a bit longer, each time smiling a bit wider.

In that moment, I saw it clearly: this wasn't just surfing. It was resilience in action. The waves may knock you down. But you rise, paddle back, reposition, wait for the next swell—and try again. You learn to duck, dive, and wait for the right moment to ride what could have crushed you.

We ended those beach days sun-kissed, salty, and deeply satisfied. The beach wasn't just a field trip. It was a declaration: we can learn anywhere. The world is our classroom. And this windswept, salt-kissed coast—with all its unpredictability—was the perfect teacher.

Author's Reflection

Some of our most profound learning moments have occurred outside the confines of traditional classrooms. On those sunlit days at the beach, my daughters weren't merely playing—they were engaging in hands-on science, testing their physical limits, and cultivating resilience.

Research underscores the benefits of such nature-based learning experiences. A systematic review by Johnstone et al. found positive associations between nature-based early childhood education and children's self-regulation, social skills, and cognitive development. The study highlighted that immersive interactions with natural environments can foster diverse types of play, enhance creativity, and promote prosocial behaviors.

By choosing to learn amidst the waves and sand, we weren't deviating from education—we were enriching it. Nature became both our classroom and our teacher, offering lessons that textbooks alone could never convey. Lessons that connect you—to nature, to each other, to something bigger than any curriculum could contain.

I saw my children differently at the beach. Freer. Bolder. Unfazed by failure and fueled by wonder. And I saw myself differently too—not as the orchestrator of every lesson, but as a facilitator of awe.

25. Johnstone, A., Tink, L. N., & Ball, G. D. C. (2022). Nature-based early childhood education and children's social, emotional, and cognitive development: A mixed-methods systematic review. Frontiers in Public Health, 10, 9142068. https://doi.org/10.3389/fpubh.2022.9142068

Reader Reflections

What nature-based learning environments seem to unlock your child's curiosity or confidence? Is it the beach, the woods, a museum, or somewhere else entirely?

How have you witnessed your child thrive in unexpected environments? What did that moment teach you as the educator?

Reader Reflections

Write about how you want to incorporate nature, movement, or spontaneity into your homeschool rhythm. What barriers stand in the way—and what creative solutions might help?

"Excellence is not an act, but a habit. The things you do the most are the things you will do best."

~ MARVA COLLINS

DISCIPLINE, ATHLETICISM & SPORTSMANSHIP
BASKETBALL DAD
MOVEMENT BUILDS MORE THAN MUSCLES

Discipline Athleticism & Sportsmanship

Movement Builds More Than Muscles

In our homeschool, physical education wasn't just a subject—it was a rhythm of life. Whether shooting free throws on the court, spinning pirouettes in the dance studio, butterfly strokes in the pool, or racing down the rink in roller skates, my girls discovered that movement builds more than muscles. It forms resilience, sharpens focus, and stretches the soul.

Our neighborhood's outdoor hoops became the workspace. At the court we saw sweat, laughter, and fierce competition—especially when Daddy was out there coaching. He didn't just rebound shots—he rebounded their confidence.

"Bend your knees, eyes on the rim," he'd remind them. "You don't need luck—you need form, follow-through, and repetition."

When Lizzy made her first layup over him, the whole neighborhood probably heard the commotion. That same competitive drive carried her onto a travel basketball team. I'll never forget the weekend she helped her team take home the championship trophy, grinning so wide I thought her cheeks might cramp.

She was already at the top of the three-point line—feet firm, eyes scanning. Then, as the pass sailed toward her, she stepped back. A little farther than usual.

From the sidelines, her dad's voice pierced the roar of the crowd.

"No! Not the white line, Lizzy, too far!"

But Lizzy didn't flinch. The muffled cheers and sideline rants became background noise. She set her feet. She breathed. And she let it fly.

Swish!

"OHHHHH!" we shouted together—our shock instantly flipping to awe. The entire bench erupted. The ball hadn't just gone in—it had danced through the net.

If there had been such a thing as a four-pointer, this would've been it.

The ref raised both arms high in the air for the goal sign, and Lizzy turned, calm and collected, shooting up three fingers with confidence and pride.

She made it.

Watching her shine in that golden moment, we saw the fruit of hard work, not just raw talent.

On the flip side of the court was the dance floor, where June turned discipline into art. She practiced pliés at the barre in a quiet studio with soft pink walls and polished floors. Her tap shoes clicked out rhythms late into the evening as her body learned to follow the music. Her younger sister Ari was a ballerina too—spinning, stretching, and smiling through every sore muscle.

"Look, I can do a front split, side split, and the other side split is almost there!" Ari boasted.

Dance wasn't easy. Behind every graceful step was a hundred repetitions. But it all came together on recital night.

The velvet curtain lifted. The galaxy-themed backdrop shimmered, and little dancers twirled across the stage in sparkled red tutus like glittering planets in orbit. And there, in the middle, was June—playing the quirky, whimsical solo role in "Supercalifragilisticexpialidocious." Her part? To fall asleep mid-performance, snoozing dramatically on stage while her troupe danced on.

She did it perfectly. As the music turned dreamy, she curled up center stage and let her eyes flutter shut. The crowd chuckled softly at her over-the-top slumber. The other dancers continued without her, tapping and twirling. When the final chord burst into its peppy reprise, the other girls froze—waiting, glaring toward June.

Still "asleep."

The audience held their breath.

Then—June stretched. Yawned. Rubbed her eyes. And with a twinkle of the cue music, leapt right back into formation with the widest, cheekiest grin. Her timing was flawless. The crowd burst into laughter and applause. She owned her moment. Pure, sweet magic.

And they kept working—through the sweat of hot summer day practices, the sting of blisters and muscle cramps, and the quiet heartbreak of missed steps or lost games. They kept showing up. They kept moving. Because in our homeschool, PE wasn't about perfection—it was about persistence. About putting your heart into something and watching your body and mind rise to meet the challenge.

We danced. We dribbled. We jumped, twirled, sprinted, and sometimes crawled to the finish. PE wasn't relegated to a time slot—it lived in our living room, our driveway, and every studio or sports venue we could reach.

We learned that the body is an instrument. And like any instrument, it needs tuning, training, and a lot of love.

Author's Reflection

The myth that homeschoolers don't "do" PE is just that—a myth. According to the Centers for Disease Control and Prevention (CDC), children ages 6–17 should get at least 60 minutes of physical activity daily, and this activity supports better focus, academic achievement, and emotional regulation.[23] Our physical education goals were never about checking a course box, nor becoming an all-star player or prima ballerina—they were about honoring the whole child. Physical learning was as important as reading or writing.

In a 2021 peer-reviewed study published in the Journal of School Health, researchers found that homeschool families who prioritize physical activity often implement diverse strategies—from organized sports to parent-led routines—and achieve comparable or even higher activity levels than public school counterparts.[24] It's about flexibility and intentionality, not infrastructure.

We used it all. Neighborhood basketball drills. Dance studio instruction. And indoor movement videos on rainy days. We rotated through Kids Yoga, dance breaks, and HIIT videos for kids. When energy ran high and we needed a break from books, we made space in the living room and pressed play.

I watched my daughters gain confidence through sports and dance, not just strength. I saw them develop social skills on teams and perseverance in ballet class. I witnessed grit when they practiced the same move over and over until their bodies finally agreed with their minds.

Daddy's role was irreplaceable—he was both coach and cheerleader. His steady presence on the basketball court and at performances meant the world to the girls. It also reminded me that physical education is a family affair. It's in the way we show up, how we model effort, and the joy we find in every leap and layup.

We didn't need a gym to get stronger. We just needed each other—and the will to keep moving forward.

23. Centers for Disease Control and Prevention. (2022). Physical activity facts. U.S. Department of Health and Human Services. https://www.cdc.gov/healthyschools/physicalactivity/facts.htm

24. Wenner, J. A., & Yan, Z. (2021). Physical activity patterns and practices in homeschooling families: Results from a national survey. Journal of School Health, 91(6), 488–495. https://doi.org/10.1111/josh.13027

Reader Reflections

What are your goals for physical education in your homeschool or learning environment this year? Sports, dance, general PE?

How do you model physical wellness as a family? Are there any physical challenges that present opportunities for modifications?

Reader Reflections

What opportunities in your neighborhood could you use to turn casual movement into a meaningful PE routine?

What life lessons has your child learned through athletic or artistic movement?

"Tell me and I forget. Teach me and I remember. Involve me and I learn."

~ BENJAMIN FRANKLIN

BAKING UP
BRILLIANCE
LEARNING WITH ART
AND PASSION

Baking Up Brilliance

Learning with Art and Passion

Baking isn't just a hobby in our family—it's a passion.

But more than that, it's a legacy. June's love for the kitchen didn't start with her. It didn't even start with me.

It was passed down through generational ideation—a quiet, powerful tradition of women teaching with their hands, their hearts, and a dusting of flour.

My own baking education began in Grandma's kitchen.

I stood beside her, wide-eyed and obedient, watching every flick of her wrist and measuring cup. I emulated her precision. I memorized her rhythm. I followed instructions not just because they were steps in a recipe—but because they were lessons in love.

She taught me the staples: Banana Bread, Red Velvet, German chocolate cake. But some things she kept close. The peach cobbler and lemon meringue? Only for special occasions. I never did get those recipes—but I got something better.

I learned. And she taught me.

And now, I pass it down to my daughters, just like she passed it to me—side by side at the counter, stirring, measuring, laughing, and discovering something far richer than sugar or spice.

June's passion started early. From the time she was barely tall enough to peek over the countertop, she's been right by my side in the kitchen—measuring, mixing, and making magic happen in the oven.

Looking up at me she'd ask, "Can I crack the eggs, Mommy? Please?"

I'd look back at her, trying to conceal my secret of not wanting to make a mess or have to dig out egg shells. So I show her, "watch me first." And then I guide her hands to crack one egg. Because, how can she learn if she does not do?

One Christmas, she received Disney's Tiana Cookbook from her favorite aunt. Flipping through the recipes and finished product photos, she'd found her prize.

"I want to make Louis's Alligator Cake!" she exclaimed.

I'd find the book propped open to that page—her silent but persistent signal that the time had come. I dug out the bundt pans and bread carving knives, then made a dollar store run for green gumballs and gumdrops.

We rolled up our sleeves, measured flour, butter, and sugar, and poured heart and soul into the task.

The result? A cake that didn't quite match the picture—but looked hilariously, and adorably, like a real cartoon alligator. June beamed with pride. And the best part? Sharing our sweet creation with our homeschool friends at a "See You Later, Alligator" farewell party. We were preparing for our big move back to Florida, and the cake made the sendoff all the sweeter.

Baking has become a staple in our homeschool life—a creative ritual we return to again and again. Whether it's a solo bake with June or a full-blown Family Bake-Off Challenge, there's learning happening in every scoop and sprinkle.

During the Bake Offs, each daughter would pick a recipe or a kit and the kitchen transforms into a flour-dusted lab of laughter and science.

"Hey! That's my spatula!" exclaimed June.

"Who has the baking soda?" Lizzy demanded.

"I need more sprinkles!" Ari chimed.

And when they'd argue who's bake would be the best, I'd reply, "We'll let Daddy be the judge," knowing he would give each of them 1st place in their own category.

Yes, it's messy. Yes, it's loud. But it's also a classroom of joy.

We've even used baking to explore world cultures—visiting the Netherlands, Italy, and Sweden through Baketivity's Euro Trip baking camp. Each kit delivered a geography lesson alongside a delicious dish. We discussed ingredients, traditions, and flags while folding batter and shaping dough. Talk about STEAM in action!

Sometimes, the girls follow the recipe to the letter. Other times, we modify it—"Let's double the vanilla."

"Let's swap out the raisins for chocolate chips."

"Let's make the bunny cookies fuzzy with coconut for fur!"

Along the way, they learn problem-solving, patience, teamwork, and how to clean a kitchen after a creative whirlwind. That part is non-negotiable.

"You bake it, you clean it," I say, handing over the sponge.

And best of all? They're developing their passions. For June, baking isn't just a hobby —it's a channel for focus, confidence, and self-expression. In this house, baking is school.

Her dedication even earned her an invitation to audition for a popular children's baking competition show. She was ecstatic—ready to rise to the challenge. Me? Not so much, once I saw the portfolio requirements: macarons? Éclairs? Fondant-sculpted cakes?! I had never baked anything that fancy. I'm more of a "Grandma's classics" kind of baker. French patisserie was not in my wheelhouse.

And just like that, I caught myself. I was about to clip June's wings—dampen her enthusiasm and willingness to take risks—simply because I didn't have the experience. But there are too many tools at our fingertips now to use inexperience as an excuse not to learn. So, I locked in. I scoured YouTube tutorials for kid-friendly, doable recipes and helped her prep like a pro.

After watching, rewatching, pausing, and playing the videos, she gave her full attention to every step: separating eggs, whipping stiff peaks, piping perfect circles, and flavoring her cotton candy pink filling. She nailed it. Her macarons were truly something to be proud of!

We plated her delicate creations, poured some tea into our dainty set, and sat poolside for an afternoon of "tea and crumpets" in true celebratory fashion.

She took the first bite and beamed wide-eyed. "These are actually really good!"

"Of course they are!" I agreed as I nodded for everyone else to dig in.

"Wow, June these are amazing!" exclaimed her sisters.

Honestly, we didn't need the show. It was never about the competition. It was a journey of self-discovery. And it turned out to be one of the most engaging and empowering learning experiences June had ever had.

Author's Reflection

Baking is more than a fun break from formal lessons—it's an interdisciplinary masterclass. In our kitchen, my daughters develop mathematical fluency, scientific inquiry, fine motor coordination, and emotional regulation. And the results are delicious.

Educational research backs what we've lived. According to Gerde et al., activities like cooking support young children's development in early science and mathematics when paired with dialogue, measurement, and prediction.[26] When children measure ingredients or adjust recipes, they're engaging in authentic applications of addition, fractions, and ratios. They're also exercising executive functioning—following sequences, managing time, and planning ahead.

Additionally, experiential learning theory emphasizes that knowledge is most durable when tied to hands-on activity and personal relevance.[27] Our baking projects are not just lessons—they are shared experiences that integrate sensory memory, emotional bonding, and purposeful play.

June's favorite bake kits have also empowered independent learning. With kits like I'm the Chef Too! or Baketivity, she follows step-by-step instructions, reflects on her successes, and adapts when things don't go as planned. These are foundational life skills, and they're being cultivated through cupcakes!

And perhaps most importantly, we're encouraging our children to develop and pursue their interests. When kids are invited to explore what excites them, learning becomes joyful and meaningful.[28] For June, baking is a form of play and purpose—a gateway to confidence, creativity, and maybe even a future career.

26. Gerde, H. K., Schachter, R. E., & Wasik, B. A. (2013). Using cooking to teach early math and science skills in preschool. YC: Young Children, 68(3), 30–36.

27. Kolb, D. A. (1984). Experiential learning: Experience as the source of learning and development. Prentice-Hall.

28. Tomlinson, C. A., & Moon, T. R. (2013). Assessment and student success in a differentiated classroom. ASCD.

Reader Reflections

Make a list of activities that have sparked deep interest. How can you nurture those passions and turn them into learning opportunities across subjects?

How might baking or cooking serve as an integrated STEAM experience and character development in your family or classroom?

READER REFLECTIONS

Have you ever found yourself hesitating to dive into something new because of your own inexperience? What helped you move forward—or what held you back?

"You are not behind. You are exactly where you need to be. Everything is unfolding."

~ ALEX ELLE

GRACE IN THE MEANTIME
RESPONDING TO STRUGGLE WITH PRESENCE AND PURPOSE

Grace in the Meantime

Responding to Frustrations with Presence and Purpose

Not every homeschool day is perfect. In fact, many days feel anything but. There are mornings when attitudes sour, lessons derail, and the weight of everything—school, home, motherhood—lands right in the center of your chest.

The sink was full of dishes. There were three baskets of laundry waiting to be folded—again. I had stepped on a hair bead, stubbed my toe on a the piano bench, and we hadn't even finished handwriting. I had hoped to review place value with June, work through Ari's cut-and-glue activity, and check Lizzy's grammar—but instead, I found myself on the kitchen floor, eyes closed, breathing through tears of frustration that weren't entirely my daughter's.

June sat across from me at the table, pencil clutched tight.

She groaned. "It's too hard!"

Then slammed the pencil down for the third time.

Her eyes filled. "I can't do it!" she cried, eyes brimming.

And she was right. That moment was hard. For both of us.

She was overwhelmed by her assignment. I was overwhelmed by everything else—the mess, the mental load, the noise, the undone-ness of it all. And right then, I had a choice: to push through and force the lesson... or to pause and be present.

So I sat. Right there on the tile floor beside the untouched laundry baskets. I invited her to sit too. Ari and Lizzy, sensing the shift, joined without a word.

We sat on the living room floor, legs crossed, breathing deeply together.

"In through the nose. Out through the mouth," I whispered gently. "You are safe. You are loved. And, you can do hard things."

"But I'm not good at this," she said with quieter frustration.

"You're learning," I answered. "That's what matters."

And then we talked—not about math—but about frustration, expectations, and what it means to learn something hard. Because what we needed more than math was grace—for her learning curve, and for my limits.

Homeschooling is often romanticized—color-coded schedules, nature walks, picture-perfect crafts—but the truth is, some days feel like an unraveling. It's hair day and the sink is full dirty dishes. The laundry is never-ending. The toddler spills something sticky. The preteen sighs with attitude. You question whether you're enough—whether you're doing any of it right.

But grace meets us right there—in the meantime.

It doesn't scold. It sits with us. It says: You don't have to be perfect to be purposeful.

It reminds us that the value of a day isn't measured by how much we complete, but by how we connect. It's not about checking every box. It's about showing up for our children and ourselves, especially when emotions run high and patience runs thin.

That afternoon, we didn't finish the lesson the way I intended. But we ended it better than we started—calmer, connected, and reminded that learning includes emotional regulation, empathy, and resilience. That was the lesson.

And you know what? The dishes eventually got done. The laundry too, by the next day.

But the peace we practiced that day? That's what stayed with us. That day wasn't lost. It was redeemed.

Over time, we learned to build grace into our homeschool rhythm. We recognized when breaks were needed. We forgave clumsy words. We celebrated small wins. We learned to move—not with rigid perfection—but with flexibility, kindness, and trust.

Grace in motion looks like adjusting the plan without shame. It looks like giving extra time when mastery doesn't come quickly. It looks like seeing your child, not just the curriculum.

And maybe most importantly, it looks like offering the same grace to yourself.

Author's Reflection

I've come to see that homeschooling isn't just about academics—it's about emotional literacy and learning how to learn.

Choosing to take a breath instead of enforcing a deadline didn't mean I lowered expectations. It meant I aligned with my daughter's real needs in the moment. As ASCD reminds us, we communicate expectations not just through what we ask for, but through how we respond—our tone, our empathy, and our patience.[29] Grace is a form of high expectation. It says, "You're worth slowing down for. I believe in your ability to try again."

Research supports that affective learning is essential for the growth of gifted children, who often experience intensities and perfectionism in ways that overwhelm their development. When we teach them to self-regulate, reflect, and recover, we give them lifelong tools for success.[30]

Research also affirms that the emotional lives of gifted learners deserve attention. According to recent findings, social-emotional development is essential for building resilience and motivation.[31] These moments—breathing together, re-centering, choosing presence—are not interruptions to learning. They are the learning. They teach perseverance, regulation, and recovery.

And there's more. Moments like this, where we pause and refocus, are also metacognitive lessons in disguise. According to Wilson and Conyers, teaching students about the brain's capacity to grow and how to reflect on their learning process improves motivation and long-term achievement.[32] I didn't need a worksheet to teach perseverance—I guided her to experience it. Through breath. Through calm. Through trying again.

Homeschooling allows us to respond in real time—to treat the child in front of us as a whole person. And when I model grace, I teach my daughters that it's okay to pause, to feel, and to try again. That is success.

Growth isn't always visible in a worksheet. Sometimes it's in a quiet sigh, a fresh try, or a softened spirit. Grace in motion means showing up for our children with high expectations and the compassionate presence to guide them through the hard parts. That's the kind of learning that lasts.

29. ASCD. (2023). Are you communicating high expectations? Retrieved from https://www.ascd.org/el/articles/are-you-communicating-high-expectations

30. Manning, S. (2023). How effectively are the social-emotional needs of gifted students being met? [Unpublished manuscript].

31. Ibid.

32. Wilson, D., & Conyers, M. (2016). Teaching students to drive their brains.

Reader Reflections

When do you most often feel like you've "failed" during the homeschool day, and how can you show yourself grace in those moments?

Reflect on your own reactions to mistakes and struggles. What messages are your children learning from your tone and your presence?

Reader Reflections

Make a list of calming tools, habits, cues, or strategies that can you establish to help your child reset when emotions run high?

"One good thing about music, when it hits you, you feel no pain."

~ BOB MARLEY

THE SOUND OF GROWTH
MUSIC AS A PATH TO WHOLE-CHILD DEVELOPMENT

The Sound of Growth

Music as a Path to Whole-Child Development

I'll be honest: I can't sing, dance well, or play a single instrument with any confidence. Music wasn't a natural talent I brought to the homeschool table. But I wanted more for my girls—I wanted them to explore every avenue of creativity, including the ones I never traveled myself.

So we turned up the volume on something new.

We discovered an online music program, a colorful, self-paced, pre-recorded streaming curriculum designed especially for young learners. I didn't have to be a music teacher. I just had to press play and trust the process. The lessons were inviting, vibrant, and developmentally appropriate—designed for learners with big energy and wide eyes.

The first day we tried it, I laid the instruments out on the rug and queued up the lesson.

"Wait, ok, so these sticker colors match the notes on the screen?" June said, pointing to the red C on her xylophone.

Ari was ready to bang away on the desk bells.

Lizzy, on piano, tilted her head. "I think I got this—watch me!"

We pressed play. The instructor began singing.

"Red C, red C, red C!"

They looked at their instruments, then back to the screen. Then—ding! ding! Ding!

"We should start a band!" Lizzy was pumped up!

I raised my hands like a conductor. "One more time!" I'd exclaim on the eight count so they would play it again without missing a beat.

The living room turned into our music studio.

Handbells. Xylophones. An electronic keyboard. Music stands we'd found secondhand.

What began as occasional screen time evolved into a full-blown music appreciation and performance experience. The girls learned to read rhythms, follow melodies, and perform collaboratively.

The Christmas recital was the highlight. Decked out in white dresses and bows, they performed together—one on the bells, one on keys and vocals, the other on xylophone — with a decorated tree twinkling behind them. It wasn't just cute—it was powerful. They were proud. They were prepared. They were learning to listen to each other, stay in sync, and perform with confidence.

And that's what music gave us: not just notes and beats, but discipline, focus, collaboration, and joy. Beyond the performances, we deepened our understanding of sound through a cross-subject study: We explored the science of sound through worksheets and homemade experiments. We watched movie musicals and analyzed how songs support story and emotion. We linked music to math (patterns and counting), language arts (lyrics and rhyme), and even history (through cultural studies and composers).

We weren't just learning music—we were learning through music.

My girls began identifying notes, playing melodies, and even writing their own melodies. I never imagined we'd have a music program this rich and meaningful in our homeschool, especially one I could successfully lead without a musical background.

And yet here we were—making joyful noise and real progress.

Author's Reflection

When we first began integrating music into our homeschool, I wasn't sure how it would go. I'm not musically trained, and I worried that my own limitations might stifle their experience. But what I quickly realized is that I didn't have to be an expert—I just had to provide opportunity, structure, and space for joy.

What unfolded through the Prodigies program and our multi-sensory learning approach was more than just musical knowledge. It was rhythm, coordination, attention, perseverance, and pride. My daughters weren't just learning notes—they were learning how to collaborate, express, and persist.

Research affirms that when students are given access to creative, multi-modal experiences, engagement and retention improve significantly. The Florida Department of Education highlights that music and the arts support motivational competency and emotional connection, two keys to long-term learning and confidence.[33]

But it was more than engagement. I also saw emotional growth. Music became a form of social-emotional learning—a place to build confidence, process emotion, and celebrate small victories. Gifted learners, in particular, benefit from these affective domains of instruction. As Manning notes, when students are encouraged to explore their identities, interests, and emotional responses through creative expression, their sense of self and motivation flourish.[34]

Even now, I can still hear the harmonies of that first Christmas recital. Not just in the bells and keys—but in their laughter, their focus, their excitement. That was the sound of growth.

We're still discovering what paths each of my daughters will take. But music has become more than a subject—it's a metaphor for learning itself: layered, expressive, sometimes unpredictable, and always richer when shared. And if this journey has taught me anything, it's that every child deserves a chance to find their rhythm—and to feel proud when they do. You don't have to be a musician to make music part of your homeschool. You just have to be open to learning alongside your kids—and willing to get a little noisy along the way.

33. Florida Department of Education. (2022). Effective instructional practices to support student engagement and motivation.

34. Manning, S. (2023). How effectively are the social-emotional needs of gifted students being met?

Reader Reflections

What subjects have you hesitated to explore because you feel unqualified?

Write about your earliest memory of music and how it shaped your view of learning. How might that memory impact the way you teach it?

Reader Reflections

List three ways you could bring more music into your homeschool for joy, focus, or growth through music. From simple: clapping games, singalongs, rhythm sticks, or storybook songs to music curriculum platforms or lessons.

What is one musical experience—live or virtual—you'd like to share with your children this year? How might you prepare for it together?

"It's not about being perfect. It's not about where you come from. It's about who you want to be."

~ **MICHELLE OBAMA**

GLIDE INTO GROWTH
EMBRACING NEW MOVES AND A NEW MINDSET

Glide into Growth

Embracing New Moves and a New Mindset

There's something magical about the sound of skates carving across fresh ice—like a soft whisper of courage under every step. Our ice skating journey didn't begin beneath the dazzling lights of Rockefeller Center, but in a much humbler setting: a local rink with fluorescent lighting, a rented locker bin, and cold toes.

And that was just fine.

We didn't start with spins, turns, or elegant posture. We started with wobbly ankles, skate aid stabilizers, and a few hard tumbles. Lizzy, June, and Ari each approached the ice in their own unique way.

Lizzy stepped on the ice with careful, hesitant steps while gripping the wall, but refused to use the skate aide. "That's for babies," she declined.

June continued to hold the wall like it was her lifeline. "I'm not letting go," she declared. "The ice is so slippery!"

Ari glided past her with the skate aid, wobbling.

It wasn't about skill. It was about willingness.

I had never ice skated before, so this was just as much my lesson as it was theirs. Each practice became its own lesson. We bundled up and made our way to the rink with anticipation and butterflies. They learned to lace up their own skates, stand up after falling, and encourage one another through slips and near spills. Some days, progress looked like a single confident glide. Other days, it looked like laughter after a tumble. But every session left us closer than before.

As homeschool parents, we've always believed that exposure matters more than perfection. We don't wait until everything is aligned to begin—we start where we are, even if that means learning in public, failing forward, and finding joy in baby steps.

Then came the big moment—skating at Rockefeller Center under the sparkling holiday lights. The city buzzed around us, but our focus was on the ice. They were ready with their pink puffy jackets zipped tight.

June grabbed my hand. "What if I fall in front of everyone?"

"You might," I said with a smile. "But then you'll get back up. Just like always. But we can hold hands until you're comfortable."

And there we were, skating side-by-side like pros. Not Olympic athletes—but persistent, joyful, proud daughters who had taken something intimidating and turned it into delight.

We didn't go to New York just to skate. We went to mark something: the process, the practice, the perseverance. To show our girls that growth isn't a straight line, but a spiral of tries, tumbles, and triumphs. Love, culture, and identity were there too. During visits sweet grandma, uncle, and cousins share their own stories of tenacity and resilience.

In our homeschool, the goal isn't to pick a single passion early and commit forever. It's to sample the possibilities. Today it's skating. Tomorrow it might be violin, coding, horseback riding, or marine biology. We're exploring the menu of life—and collecting confidence with every taste.

The real lesson?

You don't have to be perfect to be powerful. You just have to be willing.

Author's Reflection

Sometimes, the most profound lessons come not from textbooks, but from trying something brand new with shaking knees and hopeful hearts.

When we stepped onto the ice, we weren't trying to master a skill—we were embracing the process of becoming learners again. That's what I've come to value most in this journey: growth over mastery. Ice skating was unfamiliar territory, but it became a backdrop for one of our most important lessons—perseverance.

Research on growth mindset shows that students thrive when they believe their abilities can develop through effort, strategy, and reflection.[35] I saw this every time my daughters stood up after a fall or skated one inch farther than the week before. We didn't measure success by the smoothness of their glide—we measured it by the courage it took to keep going.

This experience also gave my daughters space to think about their thinking. They began to self-monitor, to notice their progress, and to develop strategies like holding arms out wide or leaning into a turn. These are signs of metacognitive growth—the ability to reflect, adjust, and take ownership of learning. According to Wilson and Conyers, helping students become aware of how they learn boosts motivation and promotes resilience.[36]

This wasn't just a skating lesson. It was a life lesson in motion. And they're carrying that mindset with them wherever they go. I'm grateful for the falls, the sore ankles, the shared cocoa after practice. Because those are the moments that shape identity, perseverance, and joy.

We're still exploring what each child's "thing" will be. Today it's skating. Tomorrow, who knows? But what matters most is that they keep exploring with open minds and brave hearts. Our goal isn't to raise perfect performers—it's to nurture persistent, reflective, joyful learners. And if they can find their footing on the ice, they can glide through anything.

35. Dweck, C. S. (2006). Mindset: The new psychology of success. Random House.

36. Wilson, D., & Conyers, M. (2016). Teaching students to drive their brains.

Reader Reflections

What activities have helped you or your child grow in confidence, even when they were difficult at first?

How do you respond when you or your child "falls down" in learning—literally or figuratively?

Reader Reflections

Can you recall a moment where growth was quiet or invisible at first, but powerful over time?

What lessons has your child learned about perseverance through physical challenges or hobbies like skating, biking, or sports?

"The wider the range of possibilities we offer children, the more intense will be their motivations and the richer their experiences."

~ **LORIS MALAGUZZI**

WILD ABOUT LEARNING
CONSERV
DIVE
INTO
NG
WONDER, RESPECT, AND PROTECT WITH
FIELD STUDY EXPERIENCES

Wild About Learning

Wonder, Respect, and Protect with Field Study Experiences

Every year, we circle the dates on our calendar with big smiles and highlighters: Homeschool Days at the St. Augustine Alligator Farm Zoological Park. It's one of our favorite expeditions —an immersive science adventure packed with conservation, curiosity, and creatures that crawl, slither, soar—and sometimes surprise you.

We buckle in, snacks packed, binoculars bouncing in backpacks, and I hit play on our go-to zoo day jingle:

"Mammals! Reptiles! Birds, amphibians and fish! But only the real ones!"

Laughter fills the car as voices sing off-key in joyful unison.

Sometimes, we cue up a podcast about endangered species or habitats. It's our pre-visit warm-up—a kind of learning soundtrack.

On these field trips, the girls transform into junior zoologists. Clipboards in hand, binoculars around their necks, and matching "Earth Day" shirts on their backs, they roam the exhibits with wide eyes and ready pencils. Each enclosure is more than just an attraction; it's a station in our outdoor classroom.

During one memorable visit, the girls paused in front of the underwater viewing tank. A massive crocodile glided past their faces, separated only by thick glass—its scaly body a silent monster beneath the surface.

"Mom… it's looking at me," June said, eyes wide.

"It hasn't blinked once," Lizzy whispered, half in awe, half in nervous giggles.

We've learned to trace the differences between alligators and crocodiles by studying skulls, skins, and the real-life reptiles just inches away.

"That one's a crocodile because its jaw comes to a point. The alligator's snout is wide and flat," Lizzy observed, pointing with certainty.

The cassowary enclosure always sparks curiosity. Dinosaur-looking turkey big bird with a crown is the best way I can describe it.

Ari peered through the glass, captivated.

“That bird has a crown! It’s the king of the birds!” she laughed, watching it pace along the fence, drawn to her bright red shirt.

And then there’s my favorite springtime exhibit: Roseate Spoonbill nesting season.

We trek the boardwalk lined with trees, transformed into a sanctuary. The pink birds perch in their nests, their spoon-shaped beaks busy feeding, flying, squawking—just being. It’s wild and peaceful all at once.

They’ve met conservation experts and handled real snake skins, shark jaws, and even live animals. One time, they each got to touch a small alligator’s bumpy tail, taking turns, fingers tracing the ridges of prehistoric design.

In another moment, they gently placed a peach slice in front of a giant tortoise and crouched down to wait.

Ari leaned in close. “He’s sniffing it... he’s sniffing...”

Then—chomp.

Ari gasped. “He ate it!”

The interaction was slow and deliberate, just like nature intended.

Some moments made us laugh out loud—like when the sloth moved surprisingly fast, or the birds gave us a little too much attention. These weren’t just visits to the zoo. They were personal encounters with ecosystems, conservation programs, and the awe of creation.

We especially appreciated the station on the Eastern Indigo Snake SAFE (Saving Animals From Extinction) program. The girls learned about the crucial role these native snakes play in the ecosystem.

“They eat venomous snakes,” the educator shared. “And they’re disappearing fast.”

The girls looked concerned.

“What can we do to help?” June asked.

They brainstormed ways we could help preserve their habitat from our own backyard like planting wildflowers and respecting nature preserves. It wasn’t just about learning science facts—it was about stewardship, responsibility, and action.

Between coloring animal habitats under shady parasols, scribbling in field journals, and talking one-on-one with wildlife educators, these days have become a cornerstone in our homeschool science journey. It's STEAM in action—Science, Technology, Engineering, Art, and Math—without a textbook in sight. Real learning. Real connection.

These are the memories that shape not only our education but our sense of responsibility, our empathy, and our bond as a family of learners.

Author's Reflection

The freedom to learn in context—in nature, in conversation, in connection—is something that just can't be replicated by worksheets alone.

Our visits to the Alligator Farm weren't just outings—they were immersive, interdisciplinary learning labs. I watched my daughters not only absorb scientific information but embody it.

The girls were scientists, writers, historians, artists, and environmental stewards, often all at once. We moved from observation to conversation, from questions to sketches, from curiosity to action. This is exactly the kind of responsive, layered learning that Universal Design for Learning encourages: creating environments where content can be accessed in a variety of ways and learning is shaped around authentic engagement.[37]

I saw different learners come alive in different ways—one child captivated by the tortoise, another asking thoughtful questions about conservation, another sketching bird wings in her journal. They weren't all doing the same thing at the same pace—and that's what made it powerful.

These aren't just memories—we're building meaning. In every touch, question, giggle, and sketch, my daughters are constructing knowledge that sticks. The zoo might be full of wild creatures, but it also unlocks something wild and wonderful in us: the drive to explore, protect, and keep learning beyond the page.

37. CAST. (2018). Universal Design for Learning guidelines.

READER REFLECTIONS

What local places or programs could serve as living classrooms for your children – zoos, nature centers, museums, botanical gardens—that you could explore with an educational lens?

In what ways have your children developed a stronger connection to nature or conservation because of hands-on experience? How did that affect their learning or empathy?

Reader Reflections

In what ways can you turn a day trip into a multi-disciplinary learning opportunity? What would you want them to see, hear, and take away from the experience?

"To listen is to
lean in, softly, with
a willingness to be
changed by what we
hear."

~ MARK NEPO

WHEN NATURE SPEAKS
BIRD
MERMAID DAD
LISTENING COMPREHENSION DEEPENS

When Nature Speaks

Listening Comprehension Deepens

On a crisp Florida morning, our homeschool journey took us to Blue Springs State Park—an oasis of natural beauty where science, wonder, and family learning flowed together like the river we came to explore. The girls had been reading, watching documentaries, and learning about ecosystems and freshwater habitats, but this was our opportunity to experience it all firsthand.

Before boarding the boat for our educational tour of the St. Johns River, we wandered the boardwalks that snaked along the spring. Interpretive signs and maps sparked curiosity, and one in particular—"What Lies Beneath"—caught Lizzy's attention.

She and her dad stood in thoughtful conversation in front of the panel.

"Daddy, how deep does the spring go?" she asked, examining the underwater topography and tracing the paths of manatees and river currents.

"This says more than 100 feet in some places," he answered. "See that cave shape? Divers explore those tunnels."

Her eyes widened.

"Would a manatee fit in there?"

"Maybe," he said. "But I think they like to stay closer to the surface—like us."

The learning had already begun.

Then came the moment we'd all been waiting for—manatee sightings. There they were, gentle giants gliding through the clear blue water with slow grace. The girls gasped and whispered excitedly, pointing and asking questions.

"How long do they hold their breath underwater?" asked June.

"Look, it's the baby and mama!" exclaimed Ari.

"They look like floating potatoes," Lizzy laughed.

But even as they joked, they stared with reverence. The manatees surfaced and sank like secrets, unbothered by the watching world.

Once aboard the pontoon boat, the journey unfolded like a living lesson in ecology. A naturalist guide pointed out herons in flight, cypress trees draped in moss, and the gator sunning on a log just feet from the boat. The girls listened intently, their eyes tracking wildlife and their hands occasionally sketching notes or matching what they saw to the wildlife guides in hand.

“That’s a great blue heron,” Lizzy observed proudly, pointing to the same bird pictured in her Florida Birds field guide. “They live near wetlands. I just read that!”

The river unfolded slowly, and so did our understanding. We weren’t racing through a unit—we were drifting in it, listening to stories of river history, water conservation, and wetlands preservation as moss swayed overhead.

The calm of the river encouraged focused listening, the gentle pace of the tour allowing our minds to absorb more than any classroom lecture could offer.

This wasn’t just a field trip. It was a full-bodied learning experience. The girls didn’t just hear—they understood. They didn’t just observe—they engaged. Listening comprehension took on new depth when paired with sensory immersion and curiosity-led dialogue. And perhaps most memorably, our family didn’t just learn together—we marveled together.

Author's Reflection

This day reminded me that some of the richest learning happens when you surrender to the experience. At Blue Springs, we weren't checking standards off a list—we were embodying them. My daughters weren't preparing for a comprehension quiz, but they were asking critical questions, making real-time inferences, and synthesizing information—all hallmarks of effective learning.

According to Rosenshine's principles of instruction, guided practice and frequent review are vital to long-term retention.[38] But what's equally important is meaningful engagement. Listening to an expert on the boat, watching wildlife in real-time, and participating in guided observation activated more than just knowledge—it activated understanding.

This trip also aligns with the 5E instructional model, particularly the "Engage" and "Explore" phases.[39] Before we even set foot on the boat, curiosity had been piqued. And once there, exploration wasn't simulated—it was real, dynamic, and emotionally resonant.

In today's educational climate, where data often drives instruction, it's easy to forget that deep learning is often sparked not in the pages of a book but in the stillness of a spring, the hush of a listening child, and the shared awe of a family.

38. Rosenshine, B. (2012). Principles of instruction: Research-based strategies that all teachers should know. American Educator, 36(1), 12–19.

39. Bybee, R. W., Taylor, J. A., Gardner, A., Van Scotter, P., Carlson Powell, J., Westbrook, A., & Landes, N. (2006). The BSCS 5E instructional model: Origins and effectiveness. Colorado Springs, CO: BSCS.

Reader Reflections

What does active listening look like in your home or learning environment?

Describe a time your child truly listened—not just to instructions, but to the world around them.

Reader Reflections

How could nature inspire a different kind of engagement for your family than indoor learning does?

"Play gives children a chance to practice what they are learning."

~ FRED ROGERS

THE POWER OF PLAY
STRATEGIC THINKING IN GAMING

The Power of Play

Strategic Thinking in Gaming

It started with a glance. During one of our regular library visits, Ari's eyes caught a chessboard already set up in the children's section. She was only six at the time, but something about those black and white squares, the silent tension of an untouched game, drew her in.

"Can you teach me how to play that?" she asked, curiosity wide-eyed and sincere.

Of course, I said yes.

We sat down right there and then. I showed her each piece—how the pawn moves slowly but steadily, how the rook slides in strong straight lines, how the knight dances in L-shapes. She absorbed the rules like a sponge, fascinated not just by what each piece could do, but why. That day, we didn't play a full game. But we built something better: the beginning of strategic thinking.

A few days later, I ordered a child-friendly chess curriculum called Story Time Chess. It was the perfect blend of learning and play. Each piece became a character with a silly story—King Shaky, who moved slowly because he was afraid of grass, and Queen Bella, bold and powerful. With each narrative, Ari deepened her understanding of the moves, now tied to a character's motivation and personality. The game became more than logic—it became a story she could follow.

When she received a Super Mario Chess set for Christmas, I was curious to see whether the lessons would translate. And they did. Even with Goombas and Princess Peach on the board instead of bishops and queens, Ari applied the same strategic principles.

She didn't play just to win. She played with intention. She disliked "unnecessary capturing" and preferred games where both players could enjoy the process. She often maneuvered her rook into unexpected corners of the board and—with a quiet grin—

"Checkmate."

I looked at the board. She was right.

I smiled. "You tricked me."

She laughed with a double eyebrow raise. "I didn't trick you mommy—I planned."

Chess became more than a pastime in our home. It became a mode of thinking. Ari learned to anticipate, plan, and pause. She learned the value of patience and observation. And I learned how games—especially ones with depth—can build brains and character alike.

When Ari quietly leans over a chessboard, scanning the field with thoughtful eyes, I know we've found a tool that's not just building her logic. It's shaping her mind one move at a time.

And chess isn't where our game-based learning stopped.

We've embraced game-schooling as a powerful curriculum companion. Over the years, we've explored: "HerStory" for women's history—spotlighting real female change-makers and sparking meaningful discussion. "Somebody" for anatomy, where body systems are explored through quirky visuals and matching cling-on stickers. "The Presidential" to walk through the voting process and electoral strategy. Electronic map and globe games to build geographic fluency with hands-on play.

Games aren't a break from learning. They are learning. In addition to content, they teach strategy, memory, collaboration, and resilience—all while keeping engagement high and joy at the center.

Sometimes, a game does what a worksheet never could.

Author's Reflection

Watching Ari's journey into chess reminded me that children don't need worksheets to develop critical thinking—they need opportunities. The desire to learn came from her, and my role was simply to follow it and shape it.

Research affirms the benefits I've seen firsthand. Studies show that chess can enhance memory, concentration, and problem-solving skills, especially in young.[40] By combining play with narrative, as Story Time Chess does, children access abstract reasoning through concrete experiences—making connections between story elements and strategic gameplay.[41] This approach mirrors the very essence of experiential learning, where meaningful interaction sparks deeper understanding.

For Ari, chess is now a form of expression. It's how she practices logic, patience, and kindness. And for me, it's proof that when we allow children to explore learning on their terms—with the right tools and encouragement—they flourish.

40. Sala, G., & Gobet, F. (2016). Do the benefits of chess instruction transfer to academic and cognitive skills? A meta-analysis. Educational Research Review, 18, 46–57. https://doi.org/10.1016/j.edurev.2016.02.002

41. Trinchero, R., & Sala, G. (2016). Chess training and mathematical problem-solving: An experiment in primary school. PLOS ONE, 11(9), e0159638. https://doi.org/10.1371/journal.pone.0159638

Reader Reflections

Make a list of games—board games, video games, storytelling games—that could become learning tools that incorporate logic, strategy, and storytelling. How might you build a unit or skill set around them?

Reflect on a time when your child surprised you with a new skill or interest. What did it reveal about their learning style or strengths?

READER REFLECTIONS

Describe how your family uses games or play-based learning in your homeschool. What have you observed about its impact?

"What gets measured gets improved."

~ PETER DRUCKER

THE PROOF IS IN THE WHOLE CHILD
UHS
UHS
HOW HOMESCHOOLING RAISED THE STANDARD

THE PROOF IS IN THE WHOLE CHILD

HOW HOMESCHOOLING RAISED THE STANDARD

The question always comes up.

“But how do you know they’re learning enough?”

I used to answer with a list of curriculum materials or a breakdown of our lesson plans. But now, I simply say:

Really, the proof is not so much in the percentile. The proof Is in the whole child and how we choose to celebrate growth and grit.

Our homeschool journey has always been about more than achievement scores—but that doesn’t mean the scores don’t tell a story. They do. The percentile ranks, the diagnostics, the results—all of these data points matter. But in our home, they’ve never been the end of the story. They are part of the tapestry of growth that we’ve celebrated with music, cake, pool parties, and zip lines. The real proof of success is in the child who loves to learn.

June, our sweet middle child, completed her kindergarten academic curriculum with unwavering dedication. To celebrate, we hosted a family ceremony right in our entryway. She wore a bright purple cap and gown, her curls bouncing as she nervously walked toward us down the hallway to the sound of “Pomp and Circumstance.”

As she approached, I leaned down and whispered, “How does it feel to graduate?”

She grinned and whispered, “I’m so nervous.”

I instantaneously had a flashforward. We were in a stadium at her college graduation, she was full-grown, 20 maybe? And she was so proud, and nervous, and she spoke those same words in her mature, yet coy, voice, “I’m so nervous.”

When we clapped and handed her a rolled-up “diploma,” she squeezed it tight and said,

“Yes! I finished homeschool!”

We all laughed.

"Not quite, sweetheart," I said. "The adventure's just getting started."

Afterward, we took her to Fish Camp, one of our favorite local restaurants, where we marveled at stuffed wildlife displays, danced to live music on the deck, and watched the waters of the St. Johns River shimmer in the background. Family surrounded her. Joy surrounded her.

When Ari finished her pre-kindergarten studies, we brought that same energy—but this time, with summer flair. We threw a pool party at our neighborhood amenity center, inviting friends from our homeschool co-op and neighbors to join us. She stood confidently in front of the pool in her pink cap and gown, a swimsuit underneath, ready to dive into her next adventure. We baked a Magic School Bus-themed coconut cake together—rich, sweet, and shaped like possibility. It read, "Seatbelts to the 1st grade!" in new Ms. Frizzle voice.

And our eldest, Lizzy, completed her 5th grade year with the grit of a girl ready for bigger things. To honor her courage, we zipped her—literally—into middle school. She chose an aerial obstacle course at the St. Augustine Alligator Farm. She walked tightropes, balanced over croc pits, and flew through the trees on a zip line. Her daring uncle and aunt strapped in beside her, harnesses clipped and helmets buckled.

"Are you sure you want to do this?" I asked as she secured her harness.

She looked through the viewing glass at the crocs lounging in the sun, and nodded.

"I was nervous yesterday," she said. "But I feel brave today."

Her uncle grinned. "Then let's do this!"

Above, they stepped off the platform—one by one—and soared.

It was bold. Brave. And wildly her. Her accomplishment wasn't just academic—it was mental, emotional, and physical resilience in action.

These were not "graduations" in the traditional sense, but that's the point. Our homeschool has never been about tradition for tradition's sake. It's been about becoming. Becoming confident, joyful, compassionate, and courageous. Becoming a thinker, a question-asker, a world explorer. Becoming whole.

And yes, along the way, we've seen the proof in the percentiles. Lizzy, June, and Ari have consistently scored in the top quartile in both reading and math across multiple assessment tools. Their diagnostic summaries show measurable growth year over year. These results reflect the intentionality, flexibility, and hands-on, research-based instruction we've cultivated. But they are not the crown. The crown is their character.

Our homeschool life has been rigorous—but joyful. Academic—but creative. Structured—but deeply human. We've studied standards, mastered skills, explored cultures, tackled science kits, and built a literary world all our own. And in the process, we've built something far greater: a foundation for life.

Author's Reflection

As an educator and mother, I once believed that data alone could tell the story of student success. But homeschooling has shifted my focus. I've come to understand that growth is not a score—it's a soul-deep transformation. It's confidence, independence, and the fire in a child's eyes when they say, "I did it."

Our celebrations aren't just cute—they're critical. Research supports the importance of meaningful recognition in cultivating intrinsic motivation, resilience, and a sense of belonging.[42] When children feel seen and valued for their effort and progress, they internalize a positive academic identity.[43] By honoring milestones—academic, emotional, and developmental—we reinforce that learning is worth celebrating.

At the same time, our curriculum and instruction were no accident. We applied research-based strategies rooted in formative assessment, differentiation, and student agency .[44] Our girls weren't just "playing school"—they were building mastery and purpose. Their percentile ranks aren't the definition of their success, but they affirm what we already know: this model works.

Ultimately, we celebrate our girls not for what they produce, but for who they become. Resilient, joyful, curious, and kind.

That's the proof I care about most.

42. Ryan, R. M., & Deci, E. L. (2000). Self-determination theory and the facilitation of intrinsic motivation, social development, and well-being. American Psychologist, 55(1), 68–78.

43. Eccles, J. S., & Wigfield, A. (2002). Motivational beliefs, values, and goals. Annual Review of Psychology, 53(1), 109–132. https://doi.org/10.1146/annurev.psych.53.100901.135153

44. Wiliam, D. (2011). Embedded formative assessment. Solution Tree Press.

Reader Reflections

How do you measure growth in your homeschool or classroom?

How do you balance the academic demands of learning with the emotional and personal development of the whole child?

Reader Reflections

What role does celebration play in reinforcing motivation, identity, and joy in your learning environment?

Reflect on how your understanding of "success" has evolved since beginning your homeschool journey.

"Education is the most powerful weapon which you can use to change the world."

~ NELSON MANDELA

FUNDING THE DREAM
5
RESOURCEFULNESS. STEWARDSHIP. CHOICE.

Funding the Dream

Resourcefulness. Stewardship. Choice.

You may be asking yourself, "How the heck are you paying for all this?"

Let me be honest with you—this journey hasn't been without its sacrifices. We've stretched, budgeted, and made intentional trade-offs. There were seasons when we gave up vacations, shopped only secondhand, and enjoyed home cooked meals over going out. Frugality was the name of the game. But, in recent years, we've also received something incredible: assistance.

And if you're reading this and wondering if it's even possible to homeschool with limited means, I want you to know—yes it is possible! While homeschooling and alternative education paths can feel like a luxury reserved for a select few— there are funding options for educational freedom for your child!

Here in Florida, we've been blessed with an evolving system of school choice scholarships. I'd argue that Florida is one of the most supportive states for educational freedom. Here, families can apply for scholarships to support private school tuition, hybrid programs, or full-time homeschooling. Through programs like the Florida Tax Credit (FTC), the Family Empowerment Scholarship (FES), and the Personalized Education Program (PEP), our family has received essential funding that has fueled learning in deeply meaningful ways.[45,46,47]

These scholarships didn't just buy "school." They opened up a whole life of learning. Let me tell you what that looks like for us:

- We've been able to purchase anatomy kits, digital microscopes, and science dissection tools that turned our kitchen into a hands-on biology lab.

- The funds allowed us to enroll in specialty courses—including culinary arts, private music lessons, surfing, ballet, and tumbling classes—activities that nurtured their physical, social, and emotional development.

- We've invested in ergonomic chairs and adjustable desks, creating a physical learning environment that supports long hours of focus, creativity, and comfort.

- We've purchased high-quality physical and online curriculum, one-on-one tutoring, and classes on demand tailored to each of our children's learning styles.

- And of course, books—so many books—to line our shelves and fuel imaginations.

We also didn't realize how far our scholarship dollars could stretch until they started traveling with us. With our Orlando Science Center membership, funded through our education scholarship, we gained access to the ASTC Passport Program—opening doors across Florida to hands-on learning at no additional cost. In Fort Myers, we visited the IMAG History & Science Center, where Lizzy built circuits while June studied water conservation models, connecting what we'd studied at home to real-world applications. On another weekend, our membership brought us to MOSH in Jacksonville, where the girls explored river ecosystems and mapped out the St. Johns watershed with wide-eyed wonder.

Through a separate AZA reciprocal zoo membership—also covered by scholarship—we visited the Brevard Zoo and the Central Florida Zoo, where Ari gleefully identified birds from our backyard nature unit, and June peppered the zookeepers with questions about animal rehabilitation. One afternoon, we lined up for giraffe feeding —Ari on tiptoes, palm outstretched, squealing as the giraffe's long, blue tongue swooped in to grab a lettuce leaf.

Later that same day, we made our way to the stingray cove, where a shallow saltwater pool shimmered with graceful motion. Lizzy, the bold one, gripped the shrimp between two fingers just as the zookeeper instructed. She dipped her hand as deep as she could, holding perfectly still, waiting for what she called a "hungry sea frisbee" to glide over and nibble it from her grasp. June stood beside her, but when the stingray approached, she panicked at the last second and flung her shrimp into the water with a squeal. Ari, more cautious, waited until the others were done, then slowly reached one fingertip to the surface—reluctantly, but bravely—gently stroking the silky, slick back of a passing ray.

These weren't just field trips—they were extensions of our curriculum, where learning leapt off the page and came to life in motion, sound, and scale.

What the scholarship really gave us was access—not just to institutions, but to experiences we wouldn't have thought possible on our own. It gave us a way to make learning mobile, relational, and deeply rooted in curiosity.

Homeschooling is not about "doing school at home." Homeschooling is about creating a vibrant, personalized experience. When we bought ergonomic chairs, it wasn't about luxury—it was about letting a child with sensory needs feel grounded and supported. When we signed up for a dance class, it wasn't about competition—it was about rhythm, self-expression, and confidence. When we ordered science kits, it wasn't about checking a credit-bearing course off the list—it was about cultivating curiosity.

We even discovered that our scholarship provider offered a local directory of approved hybrid programs, micro schools, and homeschool co-ops—some of which met just a few days per week, providing tutoring, social learning, and enrichment activities while allowing us to maintain our homeschool rhythm.

Florida isn't the only state creating access. In Texas, families now have access to a $1 billion voucher program that provides up to $10,000 per child for private school tuition and $2,000 for homeschool-related expenses. In Tennessee, a new voucher system is rolling out that allows eligible students to use public funds for private or home-based learning. Alabama has passed legislation to expand its support for families seeking alternative education paths. West Virginia's Hope Scholarship and Utah's universal ESA are examples of a growing trend across the nation—one that recognizes parents as primary decision-makers in their child's education.

And now, at the time of writing, new legislation—such as the proposed Education Credit for Children Act (ECCA)—is being considered to expand access to education savings accounts or tax credits nationwide.

When the One Big Beautiful Bill passed on July 4th 2025, it quietly embedded in the hundreds of pages a major shift in American education policy: the establishment of the first national private school voucher program. This policy introduces a new chapter in school choice—one that reaches beyond state borders and opens the door for federal dollars to follow students into private and alternative learning settings.

Families once excluded from personalized learning due to financial constraints are now being invited to the table. And that, in itself, is worth celebrating.

Author's Reflection

I didn't grow up thinking this kind of education would ever be an option. We've taken a road less traveled and recently, thanks to state funding, we haven't had to do it completely alone. These scholarships haven't just covered costs—they've validated our decision to invest in a learning lifestyle that reflects our values and our children's needs.

In the new education voucher system, individuals and corporations can earn federal tax credits for donating to nonprofit scholarship organizations. These organizations then distribute funds to eligible families to help pay for private school tuition, books, tutoring, and other educational services. It's similar in some ways to the ESA programs we've seen at the state level, especially in places like Arizona, Florida, and West Virginia. But there are key differences too—mainly in how the money flows and how it's monitored.

With state ESAs, families often receive direct control of a spending account funded with public dollars. That flexibility has allowed homeschoolers and microschool families to access a wide range of educational tools, from therapy services to STEM kits. But in this federal model, the funds are distributed through scholarship groups, and only in states that choose to participate.

That's the catch—participation is optional for states, and so is oversight. There are no federal mandates for private schools receiving these scholarships to track academic outcomes or show how students are doing. That raises questions for families who value transparency—or for parents like me who have had to weigh trust against data when choosing a school path.

Another concern is the potential for it to unintentionally further disenfranchise families from low socioeconomic backgrounds. While the goal may be to expand access, the additional stipulations in future school choice bills (like ECCA)—such as income reporting, or service provider eligibility—could end up excluding the very families who need these options the most.

Programs like Florida's current scholarship model are universal. They serve families across all income levels and all counties, with minimal barriers to entry. That accessibility is essential. Any new legislation should build on that inclusivity—not replace it. My hope is that we expand access without creating new gatekeeping structures that make personalized education less available to those with the fewest resources.

Still, it's a powerful shift. For many families, especially those in states without robust choice programs, this new option may feel like an open door.

As a homeschool ambassador and now a school leader, I see the potential here. But I also see the risk: that without clear guidelines or equitable access, this national program might replicate the same disparities it was meant to challenge. It's an evolving landscape, and I believe families and educators alike will need to stay informed, curious, and honest about what works—and who it's working for.

These scholarship programs aren't about privilege. They're about access—about recognizing that a personalized education should not be reserved for the wealthy or the lucky. They open doors for children to learn in ways that fit who they are meant to become, not limited to where they are zoned.

That's what these funds represent. Not just money—but means. A means to reach children differently. A means to reclaim agency. A means to fund the dream.

45. Florida Department of Education, "Family Empowerment Scholarship," https://www.fldoe.org/schools/school-choice/k-12-scholarship-programs/fes/.

46. Florida Department of Education, "Personalized Education Program (PEP)," https://www.fldoe.org/schools/school-choice/k-12-scholarship-programs/pep/.

47. Step Up For Students, "Florida Tax Credit Scholarship," https://www.stepupforstudents.org/scholarships/choice-scholarships/.

48. Texas Education Agency, "Texas Education Savings Account Program," https://tea.texas.gov/about-tea/news-and-multimedia/correspondence/taa-letters/house-bill-1-education-savings-accounts.

49. Tennessee Department of Education, "Education Savings Account Program," https://www.tn.gov/education/esa.html.

50. Alabama State Department of Education, "Parental Rights in Education," https://www.alabamaachieves.org/.

51. West Virginia Hope Scholarship Board, "Hope Scholarship Program," https://www.hopescholarshipwv.com/.

52. Utah State Board of Education, "Utah Fits All Scholarship Program," https://www.utahfitsall.org/.

53. Congress.gov, "H.R.531 - Education Credit for Children Act of 2023," https://www.congress.gov/bill/118th-congress/house-bill/531.

Reader Reflections

What kind of learning community—hybrid, co-op, online—might enhance your homeschool efforts?

What trade-offs are you willing to make to give your child a more personalized learning experience?

Reader Reflections

Design your ideal homeschool week—with no budget limits. Describe how you would use financial support to make learning more engaging and meaningful.

What tools, field trips, learning environments, tutors, or enrichment classes would you invest in?

Appendix A: References

ASCD. "Are You Communicating High Expectations?" ASCD, 2023. https://www.ascd.org/el/articles/are-you-communicating-high-expectations.

Bybee, Rodger W., Taylor, Joseph A., Gardner, April, Van Scotter, Patricia, Carlson Powell, Janet, Westbrook, Ann, and Landes, Nancy. The BSCS 5E Instructional Model: Origins and Effectiveness. Colorado Springs, CO: BSCS, 2006.

CAST. Universal Design for Learning Guidelines Version 2.2. 2018. http://udlguidelines.cast.org.

Centers for Disease Control and Prevention. (2022). Physical activity facts. U.S. Department of Health and Human Services. https://www.cdc.gov/healthyschools/physicalactivity/facts.htm

Denne-Bolton, Sandra. "The Dialogue Journal: A Tool for Building Better Writers." English Teaching Forum 51, no. 2 (2013): 2–11.

Dweck, Carol S. Mindset: The New Psychology of Success. New York: Random House, 2006.

Eccles, Jacquelynne S., and Allan Wigfield. "Motivational Beliefs, Values, and Goals." Annual Review of Psychology 53 (2002): 109–132. https://doi.org/10.1146/annurev.psych.53.100901.135153.

Florida Center for Reading Research. "Assessments to Inform Instruction Overview." 2022. https://fcrr.org/resources.

Florida Department of Education. "Effective Instructional Practices to Support Student Engagement and Motivation." 2022. https://www.fldoe.org.

Garmon, Mahlon A. "The Benefits of Dialogue Journals: What Prospective Teachers Say." Teacher Education Quarterly 28, no. 4 (2001): 37–50.

Gerde, Hope K., Schachter, Rachel E., and Wasik, Barbara A. "Using Cooking to Teach Early Math and Science Skills in Preschool." Young Children 68, no. 3 (2013): 30–36.

Gottlieb, Samuel, Dacher, Keltner, and Oveis, Christopher. "Awe as a Pathway to Cognitive Expansion: The Impact of Awe on Learning and Perception." Cognition and Emotion 32, no. 3 (2018): 586–593. https://doi.org/10.1080/02699931.2017.1340268.

Guterson, David. "The Role of the Parent in the Education of Gifted Students." In Handbook of Giftedness in Children, edited by Steven I. Pfeiffer, 2nd ed., 297–311. Springer, 2018. https://doi.org/10.1007/978-3-319-77004-8_19.

Harlen, Wynne, and Anne Qualter. The Teaching of Science in Primary Schools. 6th ed. London: Routledge, 2014.

Johnstone, A., Tink, L. N., & Ball, G. D. C. (2022). Nature-based early childhood education and children's social, emotional, and cognitive development: A mixed-methods systematic review. Frontiers in Public Health, 10, 9142068. https://doi.org/10.3389/fpubh.2022.9142068

Kaplan, Sandra N. Depth and Complexity: An Overview of a Framework for Thinking. Sacramento: California Department of Education, 1996.

King, LaGarrett J. "Teaching through Black History: An Overview of Black Historical Consciousness." ASSERT: The Journal of Educational Leadership and Praxis 3, no. 1 (2023): 49–64. https://assertjournal.com/index.php/assert/article/view/61/182.

Kolb, David A. Experiential Learning: Experience as the Source of Learning and Development. Englewood Cliffs, NJ: Prentice-Hall, 1984.

Macedonia, M. (2014). Bringing back the body into the mind: The role of sensorimotor activity in second language learning. Frontiers in Psychology, 5, 1407. https://doi.org/10.3389/fpsyg.2014.01407

Maker, C. June. Curriculum Development for the Gifted. Aspen Systems Corporation, 1982.

Manning, S. "How Effectively Are the Social-Emotional Needs of Gifted Students Being Met?" Unpublished manuscript, 2023.

National Research Council. Inquiry and the National Science Education Standards: A Guide for Teaching and Learning. Washington, DC: National Academies Press, 2000. https://doi.org/10.17226/9596.

Neuman, Ari, and Orit Guterman. "The Clash of Two Worldviews: A Qualitative Comparison Between School Teachers and Homeschooling Parents' Attitudes Toward Education." Issues in Educational Research 27, no. 4 (2017): 1–19. https://www.iier.org.au/iier27/neuman.html.

Reis, Sally M., and Joseph S. Renzulli. Curriculum Compacting: The Complete Guide to Modifying the Regular Curriculum for High Ability Students. Mansfield Center, CT: Creative Learning Press, 1992.

Reis, Sally M., and Joseph S. Renzulli. "Myth 1: The Gifted and Talented Constitute One Single Homogeneous Group and Giftedness Is a Way of Being That Stays in the Person over Time and Experiences." Gifted Child Quarterly 53, no. 4 (2009): 233–235. https://doi.org/10.1177/0016986209346824.

Renzulli, Joseph S., Smith, Linda H., White, Alison J., Callahan, Carolyn M., and Hartman, Robert K. Scales for Rating the Behavioral Characteristics of Superior Students (SRBCSS-R). Creative Learning Press, 2023.

Rosenshine, Barak. "Principles of Instruction: Research-Based Strategies That All Teachers Should Know." American Educator 36, no. 1 (2012): 12–19.

Ryan, Richard M., and Edward L. Deci. "Self-Determination Theory and the Facilitation of Intrinsic Motivation, Social Development, and Well-Being." American Psychologist 55, no. 1 (2000): 68–78.

Sala, Giovanni, and Fernand Gobet. "Do the Benefits of Chess Instruction Transfer to Academic and Cognitive Skills? A Meta-Analysis." Educational Research Review 18 (2016): 46–57. https://doi.org/10.1016/j.edurev.2016.02.002.

Schunk, Dale H., and Barry J. Zimmerman. "Motivation and Self-Regulated Learning: Theory, Research, and Applications." In J. T. Guthrie et al. (Eds.), Best Practices in Motivation and Literacy Instruction, 214–226. New York: Guilford Press, 2012.

Tomlinson, Carol A., and Tonya R. Moon. Assessment and Student Success in a Differentiated Classroom. Alexandria, VA: ASCD, 2013.

Trinchero, Roberto, and Giovanni Sala. "Chess Training and Mathematical Problem-Solving: An Experiment in Primary School." PLOS ONE 11, no. 9 (2016): e0159638. https://doi.org/10.1371/journal.pone.0159638.

Wenner, J. A., & Yan, Z. (2021). Physical activity patterns and practices in homeschooling families: Results from a national survey. Journal of School Health, 91(6), 488–495. https://doi.org/10.1111/josh.13027

Wiliam, Dylan. Embedded Formative Assessment. Bloomington, IN: Solution Tree Press, 2011.

Wiliam, Dylan, and Paul Black. "Inside the Black Box: Raising Standards through Classroom Assessment." Phi Delta Kappan 80, no. 2 (1998): 139–148.

Wilson, Donna, and Marcus Conyers. Teaching Students to Drive Their Brains: Metacognitive Strategies, Activities, and Lesson Ideas. Alexandria, VA: ASCD, 2016.

Appendix B: Additional Resources on School Choice and Educational Funding

These resources provide up-to-date information on state-by-state programs that support school choice, including vouchers, Education Savings Accounts (ESAs), tax-credit scholarships, and direct funding for private or home education. These tools are especially useful for families considering alternative educational models.

Alabama State Department of Education – Parental Rights in Education:
https://www.alabamaachieves.org/

Arizona Department of Education – Empowerment Scholarship Accounts:
https://www.azed.gov/esa

Congress.gov – Education Credit for Children Act (H.R.531):
https://www.congress.gov/bill/118th-congress/house-bill/531

Florida Department of Education – Family Empowerment Scholarship:
https://www.fldoe.org/schools/school-choice/k-12-scholarship-programs/fes/

Florida Department of Education – Personalized Education Program (PEP):
https://www.fldoe.org/schools/school-choice/k-12-scholarship-programs/pep/

Step Up For Students – Florida Tax Credit Scholarship:
https://www.stepupforstudents.org/scholarships/choice-scholarships/

Tennessee Department of Education – Education Savings Account Program:
https://www.tn.gov/education/esa.html

Texas Education Agency – Texas Education Savings Account Program:
https://tea.texas.gov/about-tea/news-and-multimedia/correspondence/taa-letters/house-bill-1-education-savings-accounts

Utah State Board of Education – Utah Fits All Scholarship Program:
https://www.utahfitsall.org/

West Virginia Hope Scholarship Board – Hope Scholarship Program:
https://www.hopescholarshipwv.com/

Appendix C: Educational Resources Referenced in This Book

The curricula, tools, and resources mentioned throughout this book were selected based on our personal experiences and preferences during our homeschool journey. At the time of publication, no sponsorships or endorsements were in place. Any future collaborations or partnerships will be disclosed accordingly.

Aristoplay. (1992). SomeBody: The game of human anatomy [Board game]. https://boardgamegeek.com/boardgame/3217/somebody

Baketivity. (n.d.). Baketivity – Bake and learn kits for kids. https://www.baketivity.com/

Curriculum and Culture. (n.d.). Curriculum and Culture – Diverse perspectives in history and humanities. https://www.curriculumandculture.com/

Easy Peasy Science Dissection Discoveries. (n.d.). Easy Peasy All-in-One Homeschool – Science dissection resources. https://www.allinonehomeschool.com/

Educational Insights. (n.d.). GeoSafari Talking Globe [Interactive globe]. https://www.educationalinsights.com/product/geosafari-talking-globe

Fame Master International. (n.d.). Fame Master – 4D educational puzzle toys. https://www.famemaster.com

Feminist Frequency & Underdog Games. (2022). HerStory: The game of remarkable women in history [Board game]. https://www.underdoggames.com/products/herstory

Have Fun Teaching. (n.d.). Have Fun Teaching – Educational songs, videos, and worksheets. https://www.havefunteaching.com/

Hopscotch. (n.d.). Educational songs and videos for kids [YouTube channel]. https://www.youtube.com/@HopscotchSongs

I'm the Chef Too. (n.d.). I'm the Chef Too – Educational baking kits that blend STEM and literacy. https://www.imthecheftoo.com/

KIDS Learning Tube. (n.d.). KLT – Educational videos and music for kids. https://www.kidslearningtube.com/

Know Yourself. (n.d.). Know Yourself – Bones and anatomy curriculum for children. https://knowyourself.com/

Lakeshore Learning. (n.d.). Lakeshore – Hands-on learning materials and classroom resources. https://www.lakeshorelearning.com

LeapFrog. (n.d.). LeapFrog Magic Adventures Globe [Interactive map toy]. https://www.leapfrog.com/en-us/products/magic-adventures-globe

LEGO Group. (n.d.). LEGO – Build, play, and learn. https://www.lego.com

MEL Science. (n.d.). MEL Science – Hands-on science kits for kids. https://melscience.com

Peekaboo Kidz. (n.d.). Dr. Binocs Show – Fun science videos for kids [YouTube channel]. https://www.youtube.com/c/PeekabooKidz

Prodigies. (n.d.). Prodigies Music – Colorful, accessible music curriculum for children. https://www.prodigies.com/

Storytime Chess. (n.d.). Storytime Chess – The game that teaches chess to young children. https://www.storytimechess.com

Underdog Games. (2020). The Presidential: US Presidents trivia game [Board game]. https://www.underdoggames.com/products/the-presidential

Urban Intellectuals. (n.d.). Black History Flashcards – Volumes 1–5 [Card game]. https://urbanintellectuals.com/black-history-flashcards/

Appendix D: Field Sites and Museums Visited

The following field sites and museums played a vital role in shaping some of the learning experiences shared in this book. They are organized by theme to reflect the interdisciplinary nature of our homeschool journey.

Black History, Culture, and Civil Rights

Fort Mose Historic State Park. St. Augustine, FL. https://www.floridastateparks.org/parks-and-trails/fort-mose-historic-state-park

The Best Richardson African Diaspora Literature & Culture Museum and Bookstore. St. Augustine, FL. https://www.richardsonmuseum.org

Lincolnville Museum and Cultural Center. St. Augustine, FL. https://www.lincolnvillemuseum.org

National Museum of African American History and Culture (NMAAHC). Washington, D.C. https://nmaahc.si.edu

Slave Haven Underground Railroad Museum. Memphis, TN. https://slavehavenmemphis.com

National Civil Rights Museum at the Lorraine Motel. Memphis, TN. https://www.civilrightsmuseum.org

Stax Museum of American Soul Music. Memphis, TN. https://staxmuseum.com

Science, Nature, and Environmental Exploration

Blue Spring State Park. Orange City, FL. https://www.floridastateparks.org/parks-and-trails/blue-spring-state-park

IMAG History & Science Center. Fort Myers, FL. https://www.theimag.org

Museum of Science & History (MOSH). Jacksonville, FL. https://themosh.org

Brevard Zoo. Melbourne, FL. https://brevardzoo.org

Central Florida Zoo & Botanical Gardens. Sanford, FL. https://www.centralfloridazoo.org

Orlando Science Center. Orlando, FL. https://www.osc.org/membership

Tree Hill Nature Center. Jacksonville, FL. https://www.treehill.org

Guana Tolomato Matanzas National Estuarine Research Reserve (GTMNERR). Ponte Vedra Beach, FL. https://gtmnerr.org

St. Augustine Alligator Farm Zoological Park. St. Augustine, FL. https://www.alligatorfarm.com

Kennedy Space Center Visitor Complex. Cape Canaveral, FL. https://www.kennedyspacecenter.com

Discovery Center at Murfree Spring. Murfreesboro, TN. https://explorethedc.org

Association of Science and Technology Centers (ASTC). https://www.astc.org/passport

Association of Zoos and Aquariums (AZA). https://www.aza.org/reciprocity

About the Author

Rechara Landers Groves is a Florida-certified K–6 educator, holding a Master of Science in Elementary Education and a Bachelor of Arts in Journalism. She has served as both a classroom teacher and Reading Coach in the public school system, where she was honored as a district-wide Rookie of the Year.

As a Flex Education Ambassador, Rechara's approach to learning is hands-on, holistic, and grounded in freedom—whether facilitating experiences such as dissecting cow eyes on the lanai, zip-lining over alligator pits, or scoring high on state benchmarks through nontraditional routes. She blends faith, creativity, and academic rigor to create learning experiences that nourish the whole child. As a Founding Member of the VELA Education Fund Network, she was recognized for her innovative leadership in the world of learner-centered education.

Drawing from over a decade of experience across public, private, and home education settings, Rechara brings a deeply personal and professional lens to her work. She is a mother of three girls—each with their own gifts, challenges, and dreams—whose diverse educational journeys inspired the heart of this book.

As the founder of Underground Homeschool, Rechara brings both academic training and lived experience to her work. She designs bold, real-world learning journeys that blend purpose, performance, and joy. Her story affirms that powerful learning begins at home—and that the right to choose how we learn is a freedom worth celebrating.

She is also a visionary and advocate for an upcoming Career and Technical Education hybrid school initiative designed to serve students through flexible, personalized pathways.

When she's not coaching educators, designing curriculum, facilitating lessons, or storytelling through novel projects, Rechara is likely exploring museums, enjoying the surf from the shore, or documenting the everyday magic of learning at home.

Through her writing, she invites families to reimagine what education can look like when rooted in purpose and legacy.

@theundergroundhomeschool hello@undergroundhomeschool.com

Continue the Journey with the Underground Homeschool Student Field Journal!

Learning doesn't end with the last page of a book—it lives in the questions we ask, the memories we reflect on, and the stories we continue to write.

The Underground Homeschool Student Field Journal was created to accompany this book as an interactive space for learners to draw, reflect, question, and explore. Whether you're a homeschool student, a curious kid, or a deep-thinking grown-up, this journal invites you to:

- Capture your learning in your own words and drawings
- Think deeply about the big ideas from each chapter
- Create your own field notes, just like a real explorer
- Practice freedom, joy, and voice in your learning journey

Use the journal alongside each chapter, or explore it on your own time—there's no wrong way to use it.

Because real education isn't just about information.
It's about transformation.

Find the UHS Student Field Journal wherever this book is available

Interested in Partnering?

As an educator, author, and curriculum designer, Rechara welcomes opportunities to collaborate with like-minded organizations and educational companies. If you're interested in sponsoring, partnering on family-centered learning tools, or contributing to Underground Homeschool's mission of Empowering Enriching Education, please reach out through the contact form at www.undergroundhomeschool.com.

Made in the USA
Columbia, SC
25 July 2025

7f9d8711-fabf-470e-ab53-9fff02a0eed9R01